CHURCH EMBROIDERY

By the same author:

Church Needlework (Batsford, 1961)
Creative Appliqué (Studio Vista, 1970)
Ecclesiastical Embroidery (Batsford, 1958)
Embroidery in Religion and Ceremonial (Batsford, 1981)
Ideas for Church Embroidery (Batsford, 1968)

Church
Embroidery

by

BERYL DEAN

MOWBRAY
LONDON & OXFORD

ISBN 0-264-66842-1 (hardback)
ISBN 0-264-66841-3 (paperback)

First published 1982
by A. R. Mowbray & Co. Ltd
Saint Thomas House, Becket Street
Oxford, OX1 1SJ

Phototypeset in Linotron Palatino by
Western Printing Services Ltd, Bristol

Printed in Great Britain at the
University Press, Cambridge

Acknowledgements

To those who have assisted me in many ways, and to the Revd Peter Delaney, without whose help there could have been no book – I offer my gratitude. I also want to thank the people who have taken the photographs and obtained reproductions, in particular to Judy Barry, and to Jan Beaney I am specially indebted for allowing me to include illustrations of her students' work; and I am grateful to my husband for his help.

If this book proves useful, it is the result of the happy experiences gained by teaching generations of students. To them and to future ecclesiastical embroiderers go my wishes for producing well designed, functional vestments.

B.D.

'Art serves religion
and religion feeds art'
(Susanne Langer in
Feeling and Form, Routledge & Kegan Paul)

*A triple screen which hangs
behind the Communion Table,
Cardross Church, Dunbartonshire,
designed and executed by
Hannah Frew Paterson.
The panels show the development of
life from its origins to fulfilment
in Vegetation, Minerals and
Human life.*

Contents

Introduction   *page* 7

1 Designing for church embroidery – Enlarging or
   reducing a drawing.   9

2 Symbolism, its value in design.   15

3 Liturgical Vesture—   24
     Chasubles.   29
     Stoles—Traditional and wide.   35
     Dalmatic and Tunicle.   39
     Copes.   40
     Mitres.   47

4 Soft furnishings for the church—   53
     Altar Frontals.   53
     Pulpit, Lectern and desk falls.   58
     Banners.   66
     Aumbrey Curtain.   67
     Burse and Veil.   68
     Hangings.   71
     Alms Bags.   72
     Altar Cushions.   75
     Book Covers.   78

5 Altar Linen—   81
     Fair Linen and Corporal Cloths, palls, veils, etc.   83
     White work embroidery methods.   90

6 Transferring the design to the fabric.   99
     Framing up for hand embroidery.   100

7 Embroidery Methods—   105
     Using metal threads.   105
     Quilting.   119
     Appliqué.   119
     Patchwork.   124
     Mola work.   128

8 Decorative stitchery.   131

9   Canvas work for Kneelers, Cushions, etc.—   146
        Stretching.   151
        Making up.   152

10   Machine Embroidery.   153

11   Corporate Projects and Repair Work.   165

12   A Brief Historical Sequence.   169

     Bibliography   179

     Suppliers of Materials   181

     Index   183

Introduction

The purpose of this book is to provide the amateur with a reliable, inexpensive handbook which gives practical information for the decoration and construction of church vestments and soft furnishings. There are several reasons for offering such guidance, mainly it is that few churches can afford to commission or purchase replacements as and when required. Moreover, there are now fewer commercial suppliers.

Due to the recent changes in the Liturgy and the subsequent re-ordering of the interior arrangement of the East end of the church there is an immediate call for new vestments, frontals, banners, hangings and altar linen conceived in the modern idiom.

Design for ecclesiastical purposes is influenced by current fashions in secular styles of design. This transitory nature lends liveliness and vitality which calls for the acceptance of a degree of expendability. It is regrettable that out-moded, conventional designs frequently continue long after they have ceased to communicate with the present generation.

So, to economy, and the immediacy of the design impact is added another reason for supplying practical information concerning the making of vestments and soft furnishings for the church – that is the fact that many people derive real pleasure from creating with thread and fabric, and also these people enjoy working together with others who share the same common aim, which is to produce objects of beauty for their places of worship.

If the work is to be worthy of its sacred purpose it is desirable that it should reach as high a standard as possible both in design and in execution and finish. For this ideal to be realised, the necessary specialised knowledge of design and technique must be acquired and practised. It is hoped that this book will help towards achieving these aims.

1. *Throw-over frontal for the high altar Norwich Cathedral. Designed and machine quilted by Pat Russell. Yellow, gold and tones of warm orange. (Photo Jarrold, Norwich.)*

1

Designing for Church Embroidery

During the latter part of the nineteenth and the early part of the twentieth centuries much church embroidery was dull, design-wise, due to the excessive repetition of certain features. However, when confronted with outstanding examples of the period, one has to admit that there are splendid exceptions; for example, the vestments belonging to St George's Chapel, Windsor Castle, when these are seen in their sumptuous setting. One has to learn to differentiate between what is good, when belonging to another age, and to recognise that which would be judged poor in any age.

It has taken time for a modern approach to design to be accepted, and some original ideas have been resisted, however there are forward looking churchmen who have encouraged higher standards of design and new ways of interpreting them in terms of technique. So people have become familiar with modern work and willingly recognise that it is essential to seek guidance from the expert.

Designing for the church is an interesting challenge. To be successful one must conform to certain limitations and comply with specific requirements. There are many aspects of the subject which have to be considered.

Firstly, the architectural style of the interior of the church is of the utmost importance. An informed judgement is necessary when deciding which type of present-day design can satisfactorily be introduced. Sometimes it is the stained glass windows or the form of the arches or some other feature which has inspired the artist. The great throw-over frontal, designed with much courage by Pat Russell for Norwich Cathedral has resulted in a perfect integration (1).

With the present re-ordering of the chancel there is scope for the designer to introduce exciting colours, in the form of banners and pennants. When planning the stitched decoration upon these banners also altar frontals, hangings, falls or vestments, the scale is of the utmost importance, this means the relative size of the pattern in relation to the building. As it is viewed from a distance, the subject should be large in scale. Small detail being reserved for stoles, etc. Designing for this embroidery is linked with interior decoration, so it is essential not to be afraid or

9

tentative, large shapes will 'read' from a distance and will make an impact, small ones will be lost.

The relative proportion of pattern to background, balance, originality, interest of subject – be it abstract or more representational – and suitability, these are the elements which constitute good design.

The ability to design is a fairly rare gift and, as with other professions, requires training. Large and important works for cathedrals and other places of worship are the job of a trained designer, one who understands how to plan and communicate a visual idea to other people through the arrangement of shapes, colours and technique, in terms of ecclesiastical embroidery.

But with encouragement and confidence, the ability to build up patterns can generally be developed, and many amateurs can learn how to acquire the necessary skill, thereby experiencing the satisfaction of creation.

Enlarging and Reducing

It is useful to know how to enlarge a design. To do this trace the original drawing in the corner of a large piece of tracing paper. Enclose this drawing within a rectangle (or square) and draw over it a grid composed of lines, these are lettered and numbered (*see* 2).

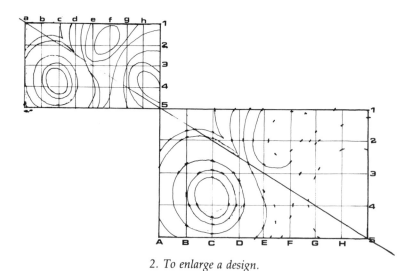

2. *To enlarge a design.*

Rule a diagonal line through the corners of the rectangle a-5, and extend this through 5 to the edge of the tracing paper. Then decide how wide the finished design is to be, and extend the bottom horizontal line of the original by this measurement, 5-1 on the diagram. At right angles to this line drop another line 1-5 to meet the diagonal a-5-5 on the diagram. Then, after measuring the enlarged vertical line 1-5, drop a vertical line from the original 1-5 to point A by this measurement. Complete the rectangle by drawing in a horizontal line from A-5.

Divide up the enlarged rectangle by exactly the same number of lines as were drawn to form the grid over the original.

Mark on these lines the points at which the design lines cross those of the grid, then join up these positions with a line drawn in pencil, so that it can be changed as necessary.

This method can be used in reverse to reduce the size of a design.

By using tracing paper for the whole process, time is saved, as this can be perforated for the transferring.

3. *To inspire design for goldwork. Jane Pemberton – Collage, composed of rolled paper, straws, gift ribbon, gold sprayed plastic tubing and plastic sheeting.*

4. *Detail of parts of an orphrey for a cope for Chester Cathedral. Cerice, pinks, reds and mauves. Designed and machine embroidered by Judy Barry and Beryl Patten. (See also page 163.)*

5. *Passion flower detail, machine embroidered by Tess Marsh.*

2

Symbolism, its value in design

Symbolism is a means of visual communication, originally pagan, many of the fundamental ideas were adapted and still persist in religion today. For example wheat or the vine. The vertical stroke which represents the Godhead in general, also symbolises power descending upon mankind from above – and the horizontal stroke in which is seen the Earth, where life flows evenly and everything moves on the same plane; when they are combined a cross is formed which was one of the earliest signs and used decoratively long before it assumed the Christian meaning. The circle, being without beginning or end, is the symbol of eternity and is ageless.

These and many other signs having an early origin, are basic elements in creative design, when their meanings are known, an extra dimension is added. But the significance of much of the highly stylistic formalisation of Byzantine Art is lost to those without the necessary understanding.

As a way of conveying a message pictorial symbols had an importance and a meaning which has, to a greater or lesser extent become lost; and for this reason their continued use lacks impact, they have become irrelevant. But where both form and meaning relate to modern design, then symbolism enriches the spiritual and the visual significance, for example the Tree of Life, the Cross, the Dove and the egg, which represents the Resurrection.

The designer of today tends to select those emblems which are good, strong forms, with which to develop, in a new way, some satisfying visual image. From age to age different signs and symbols have inspired the artist.

But some emblems have been repeated so often that they have become outworn, and the impact lost. Such an example is the Cross, the most sacred of all symbols, yet its use has thoughtlessly proliferated until it has for instance been used for the decoration of kneelers and trodden underfoot. Generally advocated is the emphasis upon one cross, probably on the altar.

Opinions differ widely concerning the inclusion of symbolism as a basis for religious design. One argument is, that if this specialised language is omitted, with it may go an integral depth of meaning, resulting in merely attractive (or otherwise) decoration. Today the approach to symbolism is seldom representa-

Some Christian symbols.

tional, it is more abstract. Shapes and form together with colour combine to convey a visual impression which creates in the mind a meaningful reaction.

On page 16 are shown an arbitrary selection of symbols some of which can well be adapted by the designer. (Books of reference for all symbols and their meanings are listed in the bibliography.)

1. The Greek Cross.
2. The Latin Cross.
3. St Andrews Cross.
4. The Chi-Ro, the Cross of Constantine.
5. The Tau Cross.
6. Fork or Furka Cross.
7. Cross crosslet.
8. An old emblem for the sun, with three rays.
9. Roman Sacred Cross.
10. The looped Tau Cross.
11. The anchor Cross, a disguised Cross.
12. The Flyfot Cross, another disguised Cross used by the early Christians.
13. The Papal Cross.
14. Interlocking triangles, the Trinity.
15. Crowned M, one emblem of the Blessed Virgin Mary.
16. Monogram of Christ.
17. A sign meaning 'Jesus Christ, the Conqueror'.
18. and 19. Signs representing the Trinity.
20. Alpha and Omega, used from very early times.
21. Symbol of the Trinity.

Some emblems associated with Saints are:
Anne: Depicted teaching the Virgin as a child to read.
Anthony: Usually shown as a venerable, bearded figure holding a Tau-shaped staff.
Barbara: Patron against lightning, fire and Thunder, she holds her tower. Patron saint of architects and builders.
Catherine of Alexandria, holds the barbed wheel of her torture, also sword. Catherine of Siena, stigmata, wears crown of thorns, holds burning heart.
Christopher: Represented as a giant holding staff and wading through a river carrying the Christ child.
Gabriel, the archangel: Sometimes wears coronet, dressed in white, holds lily. Usually has shield with Ave Maria upon it.
George: Clad in armour slashing the dragon with sword or is shown piercing it with lance.
James the Great: Is represented as a pilgrim with staff, wallet, a scallop-shell on his hat.

James the Less: A fuller's club.

John the Apostle: A younger man, chalice with snake. Eagle, book.

John the Baptist: Represented clothed in camel's hair, girdle. Lamb.

Lawrence: Wears vestments of deacon, holds grid iron.

Some decorative symbols.

Luke: Ox, usually winged. With or without book.

Mark: Lion, also winged. With or without book.

Mary the Virgin: Usual emblem the lily, also crowned M.

Mary Magdalene: Shown as a Christian penitent with flowing hair and pot of ointment.

Matthew: Represented as an Angel, he may hold a sword or money-box. Book or scroll or as angel, with sword and fish, and money bags.

Michael, the archangel; shown clad in armour, or in alb, and strikes down the dragon. Or may hold scales of justice.

Paul the Apostle: Bears a sword.

Peter the Apostle: Key or keys on chain. Also fishing net, cock or crucified upside down.

Philip the Apostle: A basket containing loaves, or long cross.

Simon the Apostle: Holds a fish, an oar, axe or saw, and book.

Ursula, crowned as a princess, holds or is transfixed by arrows. She is also sheltering her companion virgins under her cloak.

Veronica: She bears a handkerchief with the imprint of the face of Christ upon it.

A selection of symbols are illustrated on page 18:

1. The ship represents the Church riding the storms, and a safe journey with Christ.
2. The hand emerging from the clouds, together with the eye of God were employed to symbolise the first person of the Trinity. A detail from a Norman carving.
3. The six-winged angel. Gold embroidery, Byzantine.
4. Peacock represents the Resurrection, originally pagan. This example is from an early Christian monument at Athens.
5. The sign of the Cross, an early cryptogram on a gravestone.
6. An incised bronze reliquary cross, sixth century.
7. Detail showing the vine, the Redeemer. Stone carving seventh century, Asturias.
8. The Moon, the feminine principle and 8. The Sun, the male element, the symbol of the 'Son of Righteousness'. Gold embroidery, Byzantine.
9. The Dove of the Holy Spirit descending, detail from carved sarcophagus from S. Apollin are in Classe, Ravenna, fifth century.

There are many more signs and symbols, a few are here listed. Tongues or Flames of Fire, represent the coming of the Holy Ghost. Symbols of the Passion, the Chalice and Crown of Thorns, with or without the nails, are often used exclusively or together with the ladder, dice, seamless robe, cock, spear, sword, sponge, pincers, hammer, pillar, scourge, reed, rope and the thirty pieces of silver.

The Pentalpha, five pointed star is the Star of Bethlehem.

Eschallop Shell, usually associated with St James the Great, also a sign of pilgrimage.

Twelve Sheep with the Shepherd, symbolises Christ with the apostles.

The Hart or Hind – Purity of Life also piety and religious aspiration.

Three Fish – Baptism.

The Fish, Basket and Five loaves refer to the feeding of the five thousand.

A Dove or Doves drinking at the Fount signifies eternal life.

Many plants and flowers have meanings, amongst them are: The Fleur-de-Lis and later the Lily means purity and innocence, also the Virgin Mother.

The palm, a very early symbol, means victory.

The olive stands for peace and goodwill.

The Pomegranate symbolises the Tree of Life, and is usually shown with the seeds revealed.

Corn means material and temporal prosperity, and wheat the Eucharist.

Of numbers, Three represents the Trinity. Seven symbolises perfection and completion. The golden candlestick of the Jewish Temple was seven-branched.

Seven gifts of the Holy Spirit.

There are nine orders of angels in the celestial hierarchy:

Seraphim – six-winged, feathered body, sometimes a censer.

Cherubim – six-winged, feathered body marked with eyes, the hands are uplifted in adoration.

Thrones – six-winged and holding a pair of golden scales.

Dominions – four-winged and wearing a triple crown and chasuble.

Virtues – four-winged, the body covered with blue feathers, holding a sceptre.

Powers – holding a scourge and leading a devil tied by a chain.

Principalities – four-winged, holding a palm-branch in one hand and a glass vial in the other.

Archangels – two-winged, in armour, standing within a fortress and holding a sword.

Angels – wearing an alb and holding a spear. Nearby two naked souls kneel in supplication.

Colour

Of medieval origin are the meanings and sequence of the traditional Liturgical Colours. Many Cathedrals and churches possess sets of vestments and frontals in the appropriate colours for each of the Churches' seasons. Feast days and Seasons are usually observed by changes in the colour of vestments and hangings. This still obtains today, when the chasuble is worn by the celebrant and wide, long broad stoles are worn over the cassock alb by those assisting.

For the Eucharistic vestments (chasuble, stole, traditional or wide, maniple, if still in use) also burse, veil and altar hangings, the appropriate colour is generally used. Any variant of the actual colour is permissible, for example either emerald, lime or jade green.

Used in the Roman Catholic Church and by some churches in the Church of England is the colour sequence known as Western Usage.

White, cream or gold for festivals, Christmas, Easter, Ascension and sometimes for Saint's days.

Red is used at Pentecost and for feasts of martyrs.

Green for Epiphany until Septuagesima and after Trinity Sunday until the eve of Advent Sunday.

Purple, violet or blue is used for Advent, Vigils, Ember Days and Passiontide.

Black is not now used on Good Friday, All Souls' and Requiem Masses.

In the Church of England, Truro has a prescribed use and Westminster Abbey its own sequence. Generally, throughout Lent or for the first four Sundays, Lentern Array is used, this is 'off white' with stencilled or appliquéd red, blue or black symbols. For the last four Sundays Passiontide red (deep and sombre) may be used.

Attribution of colour symbolism varies from time to time and country to country.

White, being the greatest heat of metal, symbolises God. Also innocence of the soul, purity of thought and holiness of Life.

Gold or yellow which it represents, symbolises sovereignty, the sun, love, constancy, dignity and wisdom, used for confessors.

Red symbolises the colour of fire and the darker colour of blood.

Green represents the earth and nature, fruitfulness and hope, also God's provision for man's needs.

Blue signifies eternity, faith, truth and the feminine principle.

Purple, violet or blue signifies preparation or penance, also purple is for royal majesty.

Ash-colour or 'off white' is generally interpreted as unbleached linen or holland.

Black is symbolic of material and spiritual darkness.

Rose Pink, Divine love.

When planning colour schemes (quite apart from symbolic meaning) an understanding of tone value is helpful. Try putting a dark tone of a colour (i.e. navy blue) with an area of a light tone (i.e. primrose yellow) and it will result in the greatest degree of contrast (except for black and white). Two equal areas of similar tones will produce a merging when viewed from a distance, for instance purple and brown, or sky blue and lime green. The arrangement of tone values in relation to the background colour is really more important than the colour scheme when the result has to 'read' from a distance.

For those to whom this may be a new experience, it is recommended that they collect pieces of coloured paper or fabric, and try to analyse their relative values, i.e. whether dark, medium or light, then arrange them together, viewing the composition from some distance away, and noting the effect which one tone value of a colour may have upon another.

Colour schemes should always be chosen in the church in which the work will be seen, this is because the effect upon colour of both natural and artificial light varies almost incredibly.

The designer must also enquire as to the provision of lighting for the new work, and insist upon spotlight, etc., being fitted.

Designing for Ecclesiastical embroidery is beyond the scope of this book, but its relationship with symbolism can be considered.

That symbolism is the basis upon which most design in religion is based is a point requiring re-appraisal, in the past it served a purpose because the meaning ascribed to the sign illustrated an idea which was generally known, its meaning was conveyed and understood. Today many designers are introducing a form of personalised, abstract symbolism, whose meaning can only be recognised by themselves, it is well thought-out, sincere and interesting, but so much is lost because the ideas underlying the theme are not communicated unless a verbal or written explanation is available. This does not detract from the visual aspect, but an understanding of the meaning adds another dimension.

The problem presented is common to other artforms, such as ballet, where the traditional symbols or language (mime) which are commonly understood, have become outworn and the impact diminished through overexposure. This field is limited even when extended by imaginatively fresh interpretation.

Perhaps the difficulty is already in the process of being resolved by a new generation of designers of church embroidery who do not intend to be restricted by the traditional visual language. But how long will it be before the whole church accepts the wholely visual approach? Many churchmen simply do not react through vision, their minds seek satisfaction in the symbolic meaning.

3

Liturgical Vesture

'These garments, hallowed by long usage as the ceremonial dress of the Christian minister at the Holy Communion are derived from the dress worn by the Roman citizen, in the first centuries of the Christian era.' (C. E. Pocknee)

Despite recent changes some traditional vestments will probably continue in use for many more years. The full set or High-Mass set consists of chasuble, dalmatic, tunicle, two stoles, chalice and humeral veils, the burse and veil are not always used now, nor are maniples. Most churches have a set in each of the Liturgical colours.

A Low Mass set comprises chasuble, stole, burse and veil, if used. And for a Benediction the cope, stole, humeral veil, burse and veil are used, with or without the Monstrance cover.

When vesting, the priest puts on first, the *amice*, which is a rectangle of linen (6) 92 cm × 61 cm (36″ × 24″) + turnings, at the upper corners tapes 1.90 m (75″) long are attached. There is generally an embroidered apparel 51 cm × 8 cm (20″ × 3″) sewn to the top edge of the amice, which forms a collar when worn. There should be an apparel to match each set. (An apparel is a rectangle of ornamented fabric, backed and lined, and is generally detachable.)

The *Alb*, originally the long undergarment of classical dress, was made of linen, now nylon and other substitutes are used. Traditionally a decorated apparel was attached to the front and back of the skirt, above the hem, with bands at the wrists and neck.

There are albs with deep borders of embroidery around the bottom and on the sleeves, one such example is at Liverpool Roman Catholic Cathedral.

After the girdle, the priest puts on the *stole*, which traditionally, is long and about 8–10 cm wide at the bottom (7). The custom of ornamenting the stole with three crosses appears to have been unknown in England before the Reformation.

The early form of stole was long and narrow and embroidered for its whole length. In the seventeenth century onwards it became shorter and excessively splayed out towards the ends.

The Deacon's stole is straight and has a fastening.

The most sacred garment is the *chasuble*, which was in origin

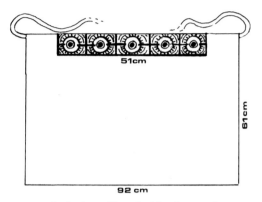

6. *Amice with embroidered apparel.*

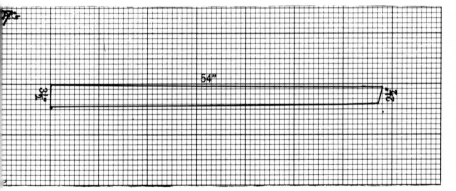

7. *Traditional stole – scale one square equals to 2 cm.*

8. *Opus anglicanum detail from the Butler-Bowden cope orphrey.*

conical, being formed by joining the two straight edges of a semicircle, a space being left for the neck, which is shaped (9). There is a return to this conical shape.

This early, long dignified chasuble (10a) underwent mutilation as a result of the introduction in the thirteenth century of the elevation of the Host, ultimately resulted in the fiddleback, which is stiff, narrow and short (10b). However, in the nineteenth century, at the Gothic revival, the chasuble regained something of its former dignity, although it now seems in retrospect, to be a skimpy garment (10c). This shape can be seen in use in many churches today, it can be identified by the too short shoulder seam, and the lack of length. The modern chasuble (10d) is long and wide, and hangs in deep folds. Plain silk, wool, cotton, and man-made fibre woven textiles are used today, as opposed to the silk or silk and velvet brocades of former times.

The detail from a fourteenth century (8) embroidery shows a bishop wearing Liturgical vestments of the Gothic period.

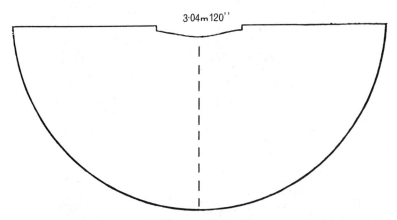

9. *The conical chasuble.*

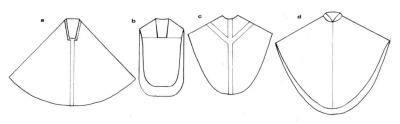

10. *The development of the chasuble.*

11. Chasuble (fiddleback). Italian early 18th century. White satin, lined with red silk. Gold embroidery using passing thread, plate etc. Bowes Museum Barnard Castle, Durham.

Altar frontal, designed and executed by Conni Eggers for Washington Cathedral, Washington, D.C. Machine appliqué on a hand-woven wool fabric.

'The Annunciation' first of a set of five panels 9' × 4'6" designed and hand embroidered by Beryl Dean, 1970, for the Rutland Chantry, St George's Chapel, Windsor Castle.

The Chasuble

The character of the decoration and its positioning upon this sacred vestment, has, through the years, changed. Sometimes it has been influenced by secular fashion and sometimes because of the construction of the chasuble.

In the Gothic period, the style was determined by both these reasons. The full semicircular chasuble had to have a central seam, therefore they tended to cover it with an embroidered orphrey (generally a vertical band of ornament) over the join. At this time it was necessary to take advantage of every opportunity to convey the Bible stories through narrative illustrations, therefore the designs of the unsurpassed 'opus anglicanum' period of embroidery were based upon representations of saints and their emblems, foliation, animals, etc. They were worked with the finest coloured silk in split stitch and in gold underside couching (8).

Later this developed into the pillar orphrey on the front and the cross on the back of the chasuble, the basic fabric of the fiddleback was usually velvet.

Many later Italian fiddleback chasubles were entirely embroidered in gold or silver threads, the design covered the whole surface. Other themes were the Virgin Mary and Child, the Crucifixion or symbols which were the main subject, and were surrounded with swirling foliated arabesques.

Silk embroidered floral designs, some symbolic, but others bearing little religious significance and closely related to secular decoration were usually worked in the Roman Catholic countries of Europe during the seventeenth and eighteenth centuries (11).

Outworn variations, combined with the lavish use of fringes and braids, have influenced some commercial vestments produced well into the twentieth century.

As its name suggests, Gothic themes characterised that nineteenth century revival, and the longer fuller chasuble reappeared with the Y cross orphrey of ancient origin. Figurative designs were embroidered in long and short stitch. At this time the work of the Pre-Raphaelites had a widespread influence towards better design.

Ecclesiastical embroidery, of which the design of the chasuble is so important a part, became dull and lacking in vitality during the first part of the twentieth century. Then, shortly before the second world war, some forward-looking churchmen were strongly influenced by the church architecture and applied decoration being carried out in Germany, Switzerland and France, and this changed the whole direction of the church arts. The effect of this renewal has had a lasting influence for good in England. Indirectly, the long full chasuble advocated today has

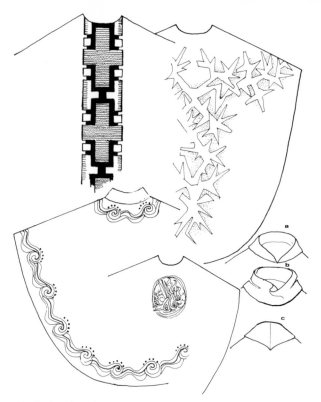

12. Embroidery for chasubles.   12A. Finishings for necklines.

been in use on the Continent for many years, so too has the lively and appropriate embroidered decoration. They are fortunate to have the advantage of the 1.63 cm wide wool, cotton, and synthetic woven fabrics, which come from Holland. In England we are limited to the wide hand woven silk, the creation of one or two weavers, and very lovely it is!

The form of the chasuble has again undergone a change, this is due to the adoption of the Westward facing celebration, which has resulted in decoration of equal interest on the back and on the front of the chasuble. Now that the chasuble is worn with the cassock-alb, the line and the draping of this vestment is even more important, the embroidery is an integral part of the long, wide, dignified garment and it is vital that the line should not be spoiled by the addition of trivial decoration, based on outmoded symbolism which bears no relation to the sculptured form of the well cut vestment.

The choice of material should be practical as well as interesting, as the chasuble has to withstand hard wear, yet it must be soft enough to drape, and the lining should not be stiff. It is made in the Liturgical colours except for ferial days. As few suitable materials 60 inches wide are obtainable, a centre seam is preferable to one across the bottom.

There are several different ways in which the embroidery can be arranged upon the chasuble (12). The choice should be made in relation to the stature of the wearer. With the modern chasuble and cassock-alb the neckline requires adaptation. (12a) shows a collar, (12b) a wide cross-cut fold, and (12c) shows the centre back join of the collar.

To work the embroidery the backing is framed up, the fabric mounted upon it, and the stitchery completed. At the finish the backing is cut away.

The collar or cross-cut fold is a necessary addition to the neckline of the chasuble when the amice is not worn with the cassock-alb. The collar is cut double, stitched and attached to the neckline of the chasuble.

13. Lettering forms an important part of design as shown in this detail from the Tidbau-Craig chasuble by Conni Eggers of Virginia.

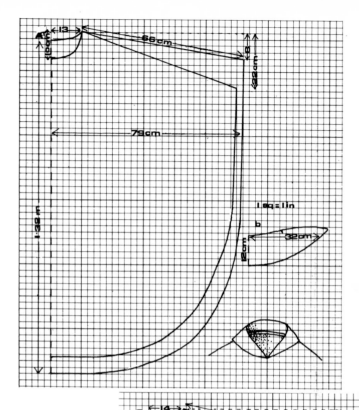

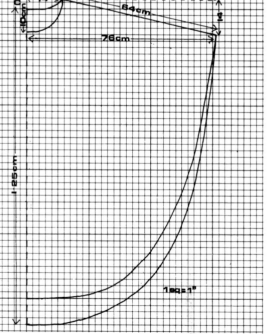

*14. 16. Chasubles
A (above); C (right);
with Collar B.*

CHASUBLE A (14)

Draw out the pattern from the graph to full size. The dotted lines represent the centre back and centre front folds and the fold of the collar pieces.

Add 2–5 cm (¾ inch) for turnings. Allow for the hem width.

When using 1.63 m fabric the centre lines are placed to the fold. For narrower widths, the centre is put to the seam.

Having cut the chasuble from the pattern, stitch the shoulder seams and press the hem, catch stitch if necessary.

Cut the lining (if used), lock the lining to the centre of the chasuble, as illustrated (15F).

Having cut out two collar pieces (14B) adding turnings, cut one piece in interlining, without turnings.

Put the two right sides of the fabric together, and the interlining to the pattern line. Stitch around the outside edge, clip the turning and turn through, to the right side, mark the centre, stitch round the neck edge and clip.

Stitch together the necklines of the chasuble and lining, clip.

Match up the centre back and front of the chasuble, the shoulder mark, and neckline with those of the collar, stitch together the neck of the vestment and of the collar.

Cut a narrow cross-cut facing, turn in the edges, put this over the neck seam to cover it, then hem in place.

CHASUBLE C (16). The Gothic Revival

The shoulder seam length and the total length can be increased.

In common with chasuble A the front is about four inches (10 cm) shorter than the back.

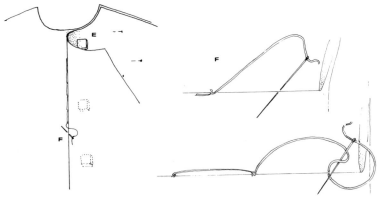

15. *Locking the centre of the lining to the centre front or back of the chasuble.*

Both chasubles can be unlined, this requires either a narrow hem, or narrow cross cut facing. A rectangle of lining material can be put over the reverse side of the embroidery, for neatening, invisibly caught to the wrong side.

To put in the lining of a lined chasuble:

When there is no collar, a piping cord is covered with cross-cut fabric, this is joined to the neck measurement. The piping is then sewn around the neck, for an unlined chasuble the edge is folded in and invisibly hemmed, when lined the edge is caught down.

1. Put the front and back of the chasuble out flatly face down (this and most of the following process also applies to lining a cope).
2. Turn up the hems, either press or use a fusable facing, or catch stitch. Start and finish at least 3 inches (8 cm) from the shoulder lines (17D).
3. Cut and seam the lining. Mark the centres (for chasubles and copes).
4. Put the lining pieces in position, matching up the centres, pin along the centres.
   Put weights on one half of the lining and fold back the other half (15E).
5. Lock the lining with tiny stitches through to the wrong side of the garment and, after pulling up the thread take a long stitch (2–3 inches). (This is much easier when there is a seam.) (15F).
6. Stitch the shoulder seams of the chasuble (17G), keeping the lining clear of the stitching. Press open the seams.

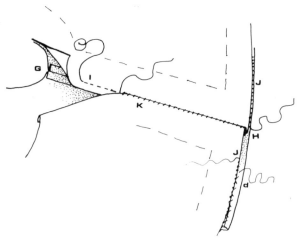

17. Lining the chasuble.

7. Complete the hems, over the seams (17D) of the chasuble.
8. Bring the back lining of the chasuble so that it lies over the seam, stitch (17J).
   Fold in a lay around the outside edge of the lining and then slip stitch or hem (17J) to the chasuble.
9. Bring the front lining over, folding in the turning, over the shoulder seam and hem (17K).
   On the lining fold in a lay around the outside edge of the front lining, and slip stitch or hem (17J).
10. At the neck line fold in the turning, clip, and hem either to the piping or the edge of the collar.

Stoles

The stole is a part of the set of Eucharistic vestments, and symbolises the priest's authority. The conventional crosses are in no way obligatory, but one cross at the back of the neck was usual. Because the stole can be observed closely, fine workmanship is appreciated, it is one instance when a small scale design is appropriate, and there is scope for interesting embroidery.

The colour and design of the stole matches the set for the season, but the Baptismal stole is white on one side and purple on the other.

The traditional Eucharistic stole is longer than the pastoral or preaching stole – preferably about 2.74 m (108 inches) or 2.44 m (136 inches) and about 7.5–9 cm (3–3½ inches) wide at the bottom. It narrows to 5.5–6.5 cm (2–2½ inches) at the neck (18A).

The long narrow stole is a uniform width of about 6.5 cm (2½ inches) and its length, from the bottom to the centre back is 1.37 m (54 inches). For a better fit, the neckline can be shaped.

THE MODERN WIDE STOLE

The stole has become increasingly important, visually; because it is worn over the new cassock-alb. As the celebrant or president of the Eucharist began to call upon more people for assistance, they tended to wear any stole which was the colour for the day. These traditional stoles had never been intended to be worn outside, so were most unsuitable. This resulted in the Church Commission recommending a new form, one which was decorative and replaced some of the colour which had been lost as a result of the changes in the vestments now used (19). These new stoles were inspired by, and based upon the beautiful old Byzantine stoles worn in the Orthodox Church of the East.

35

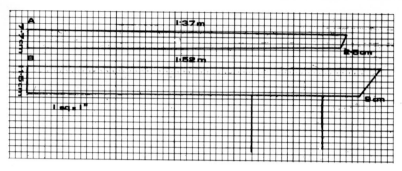

18. Pattern for traditional and broad stoles.

There is wonderful scope for the designer-embroiderer, as the decoration is either at chest level, at the bottom or covers as much of the surface as required.

These new broad stoles (18B) vary in width, from 12 cm (4½ inches) to 20 cm (8 inches) and are frequently reversible. Being worn by all those assisting in the celebration, the repetition of some design makes a splendid impact, especially as the celebrant's chasuble is a part of the same scheme.

An alternative style is cut 8 inches (20 cm) wide and is made from a soft but firm fabric, with a light interlining. The shaping around the neck is contrived by stitching two or three long tucks, from which the turnings on the back are cut away.

The method for making up the narrower traditional, and the broad new stoles is similar – it is the measurements which vary. Pattern graphs are given (18A or B).

1. Make the pattern (18A or B).
2. From the chosen fabric cut out the stole, adding turnings, seam the centre back (C.B.) join.
3. Frame up (70) the backing for the embroidery.
   On the backing arrange those areas which are to be embroidered (including joining the C.B. seam and arrange for the centre back cross, if there is one). This is tacked down, and the remainder of the stole is rolled up, it lies upon the frame, out of the way. (The design should have been transferred to the material before framing up.)
4. When completed, remove the embroidery and cut away the surplus backing, Stole B (20C), stitch the C.B. seam if not already done.
5. Cut out two pieces of interlining (dowlas, heavy linen or a substitute of sufficient weight and stiffness) to the pattern, but extend the C.Back ends of the interlining by about 6 cm.

36

6. Smooth out the stole flatly, face down on a table.
   Take the interlining, put it in position, smoothing it upwards
   toward the C.B. Repeat for the other side, allowing the ends
   to overlap, Stole A and B (20D), Stitch the interlining at the
   C.Back.

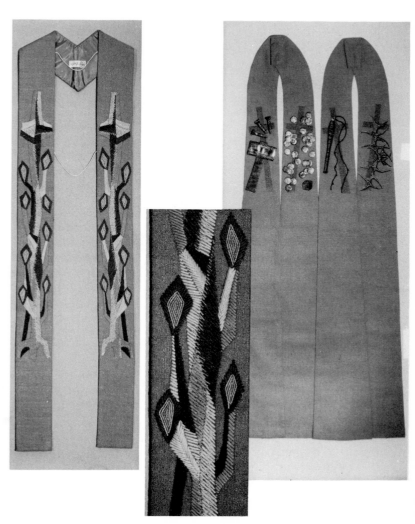

*19. The new broad stole. Green. Stitchery in wool and synthetic metal thread. By
Düster, Cologne. Passion Tide stole by Joyce Williams.*

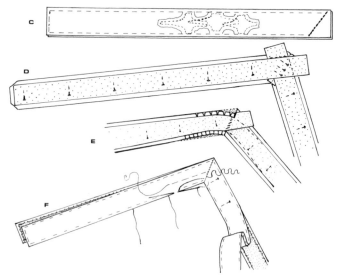

20. Making up traditional and wide stoles.

7. Re-shape the interlining at the neck. For the mitred join of the wide modern stole it is cut to the dotted pattern line, Stole B (20D). For the traditional stole, where the angle of the join is not so acute, the neckline is curved, the interlining is cut away as can be seen, Stole A (20E). Then the surplus fabric is also cut away, but leaving turnings. These being on a curve must be clipped.
   Pin and tack the interlining in place.
8. Fold the turnings of the stole over the interlining, catch stitch or herringbone (or stick with a fabric adhesive) starting at the bottom towards the C.Back. (This is in case any adjustment at the join should be necessary.) Press.
9. Cut two lining pieces, allowing turnings which are tacked. Stitch the C.B. seam, press open.
10. Match up the C.B. seams, and, working outwards from the centre, pin and tack the lining in place down the middle, Stole B (20F). For Stole A, the lining must be correspondingly shaped with the neckline of the stole.
   Starting from C.B., slip stitch, Stole B (20F) or invisibly hem the edges of the lining to the stole.

   Stole B (18) is kept in place with fine cord which is stitched to the turning before the lining is put in. They are about 8 inches (20 cm) long, the top is attached on both sides about 6 inches (15 cm) from the C.B., the second, 18 inches (46 cm) from the C.B.

Dalmatic and Tunicle

Although seldom now required, the shape and design of the *dalmatic* and *tunicle* (worn by the deacon and sub-deacon respectively) are much less rigid than they were. But there is usually some suggestion of the two vertical bands, called clavi, on the front and back of both garments. The sleeves of the dalmatic are wider (21), there might be some indication of the upper and lower apparels upon the front and back, whereas on the tunicle the sleeves are narrower (and there would be only the top apparel on the front and back). The length may be increased.

When the dalmatic and tunicle are used now, both are cut considerably longer, and the clavi are suggested by inverted pleats, this makes the garment hang in folds (22). The colour matches the rest of the set. The apparels are seldom seen with the modern shape.

To construct the pattern from the sketch is simple (23). The sides of the centre front and back panels of this dalmatic (and tunicle) are folded back, as are the corresponding edges of the

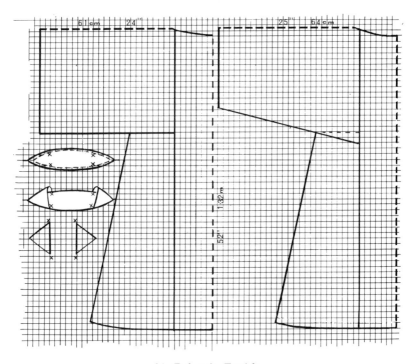

21. Dalmatic. Tunicle.

39

22. *Dalmatic or Tunicle with inverted pleats.*

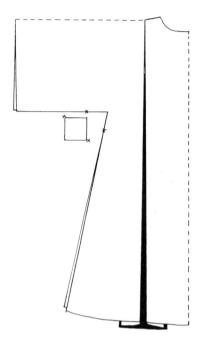

23. *Pattern for Dalmatic with pleats.*

side pieces. The inverted pleats are completed by joining to these edges the strips of contrasting colour. The sleeve ends are faced with the same colour. The small underarm gussets improve the fit. The principles for making up the chasuble apply to making up the dalmatic. The neckline could be finished with a wide cross-cut strip folded over, and the total length at the hem line can be increased.

The Cope

Copes do not form part of the Eucharistic vestments, but when worn for the celebration the colour should conform to the seasonal colour, and frequently matches that of the set. The early copes were full and graceful, with shaping at the shoulders, the orphreys were narrow, with a cowl hood. By the seventeenth century the cope had suffered degradation, the stiff orphreys had increased in width to 20 cm (8″) and the hoods (attached to the lower edge of the orphrey when of Southern European origin) were large, flat and fringed. It was not until the nineteenth century that the cope returned to its earlier, more dignified style, and the cowl hood was re-introduced.

When used on ceremonial occasions there are no restrictions upon the colour or design of copes.

Basically the cope is a semicircle (25A) fastened with a metal morse or one made from embroidered material mounted over stiffening. At the present time some shaping is preferred, as this makes for greater comfort in wear (25B).

Fabric

This should not be too heavy, nor too light in weight, as the cope should hang in deep folds. Many furnishing textiles are suitable, as are those hand-woven for the purpose as this is extra wide. If the cope is to be lined, a shiny lining is to be avoided, as this slips when worn.

Cutting

The pattern of the cope is generally placed on the fabric with the orphrey edges running parallel with the selvedge of the material. Therefore the amount of material required will correspond to this measurement, plus some extra for the piece joined across the base of the centre back to complete the semicircle. This applies to (25A and B).

Other cope patterns are placed on the fabric so that the selvedge grain runs down the centre back, either to the fold or with the selvedge edges joined together, Cope B. For all but the widest materials this necessitates joins across the front, towards the bottom of the cope. When the cope is composed of joined sections, the straight grain runs through the centre of each panel. With this type of cope a hood makes a good finish.

Positioning of the embroidery

The orphreys and hood are usually embroidered, a cowl is decorated on the inside. Or there could be a wide centre back panel of embroidery on the cope, to balance this there may be an embroidered morse of distinction. Sometimes the whole body of the cope is embroidered, but if it is made of sections, each would be embroidered (with loose threads left for lines crossing the seams), then after the joins have been finished, the incomplete lines are embroidered over the seams.

To make patterns for copes

When drawing a pattern based upon the semicircle, the amateur will find it useful to attach a pencil to a piece of string which becomes the radius (and equals the back length measurement, about 1.52 m (60″)). After fixing this to the central point, draw a half circle upon the large sheet of paper which would have been laid out flatly on the floor. Measure down 10 cm (4″) from

41

24. Dull gold, green and cream cope for the Archbishop of Canterbury by Beryl Dean. Design symbolises the wide spread influence of Canterbury and is for use in the Cathedral.

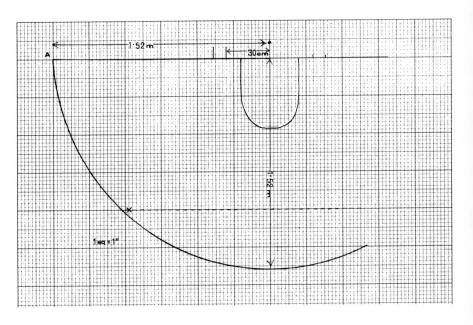

25A and B. Patterns for copes.

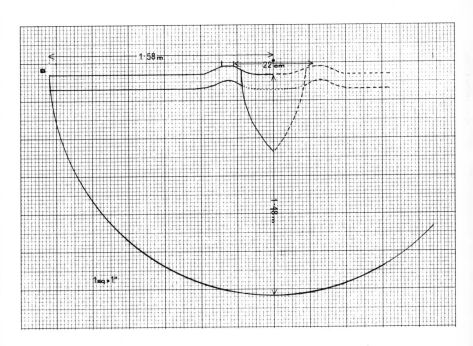

43

the central point and draw a line across the semicircle, this is the orphrey edge. Then put in a dotted line for the centre back. When this pattern has been fitted on the wearer, the position for the morse can be marked Cope A.

A simple method to make a pattern for a fitted shoulder
Cut out the semicircular cope in any odd piece of material, leave extra length around the hem line.

Mark in the centre back.

Fit this 'toile' on to the wearer, tethering the centre back with pins (26).

Make one large or two smaller darts on the shoulder line, repeat exactly on the other side.

See that the centre fronts are hanging straight down.

Mark in the new hem line.

Mark in the corrected neckline.

Mark in the position for the morse.

The addition of a hood improves this cope.

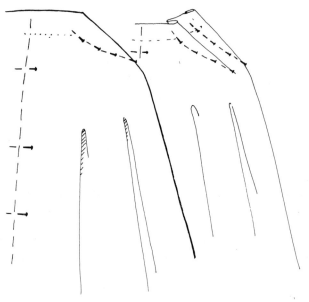

26. *Pinning 1 or 2 shoulder darts.*

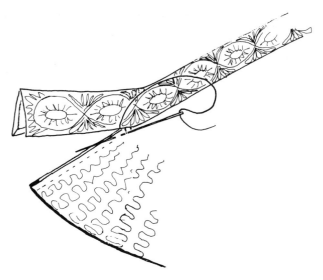

27. Sewing on the orphrey.

To make the pattern for a cope with shaped neckline and orphrey with hood

Make the pattern for the semicircular cope with a 1.52 cm (60″) back length, but let the total length of the orphrey edge measure 3.16 m. This can be seen in the graph (25B). Shape the neck.

Method of making up:

Line the body of the cope and complete the hem as for a chasuble, but do not complete the orphrey edge. Smooth the cope out flatly right side uppermost.

Make up the orphrey as for a stole, but leave one side open.

Slip the edge of the cope under the embroidered side of the orphrey, see diagram (27). Be sure to pin back the lining of the orphrey, out of the way.

Pin, tack and slip stitch with strong thread as shown in the diagram. (To do a second row of stitching gives added strength.)

Hem down the other side of the orphrey lining.

Slip the complete morse in position between the orphrey and its lining, sew strongly.

When there is no orphrey, the front edges of the cope should have a fairly heavy interlining, about 10 cm wide.

Many of the processes used in making-up a chasuble apply also to a cope.

45

Some copes are improved by the addition of a hood, the shape of which should be in character with the cope, whether it be flat or draped. But it is important to leave a wide seam allowance at the neckline, as this provides for readjustment when fitting.

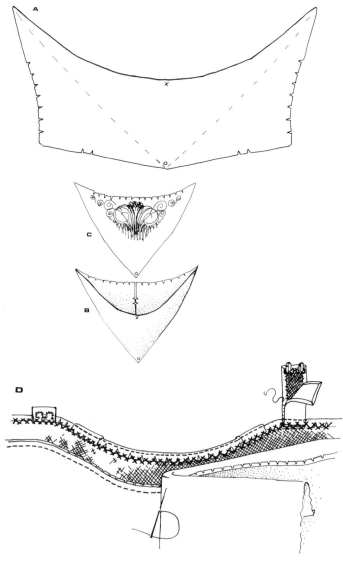

28. Making and attaching the cope hood.

The pattern of a cowl hood is made for the individual cope. The diagram (28A) shows a basic shape, and is intended to give guidance for the preparation of a pattern. Draw out a similar shape and bring together the centre seams (with two nicks) and judge the neckline so that it corresponds with the neck of the cope (28B). The interlining and the lining are cut to this pattern. But the shape of the embroidered piece for the inside of the hood (28C) is made by joining the centre seams (with the two nicks) and folding the pattern diagonally along the dotted lines; the X O marks show the centre. When the hood has been stitched and turned out, then the embroidery is tucked down inside and invisibly attached.

Attaching the hood

The lining having been invisibly locked to the reverse side of the cope fabric, was shown in the diagram (15). The neck edge of the completed hood is placed to the top of the orphrey, stitch, turn the edge over, on to the wrong side of the orphrey and catch-stitch or herringbone. It will be noticed that the turnings, being on the curve are nicked (28D). The lining is then sewn in position. This is an alternative way of attaching the lining.

The same diagram also indicates the way in which the embroidered fabric of the morse is mounted over buckram and how the cope hooks are sewn very strongly, then neatened with the lining. In the corresponding position on the opposite side is sewn a small rectangle of fabric, on which have been sewn the edges. The position of the fastening and the length must be determined during the fitting of the cope upon the wearer who, if he is vested may want the morse to fasten on the other side.

The Mitre

The head covering worn today by bishops forms the most prominent ensign of the episcopate.

There are advantages in the following method of making a mitre, one is the comparative ease with which the head size can be altered, the second being the variation in the arrangement of colours, as the gusset can be of a contrasting colour.

It is interesting to plan an alternative to the conventional decorative central orphrey with headband. Today, the mitre is less high than formerly, not more than 12 inches (31 cm). An average head measurement is 23 inches (58 or 59 cm). (The mitre may tighten up slightly in the making.)

Method:

Make the pattern to the individual head measurement (32a, b).

The front and back are made separately. Therefore the outlines

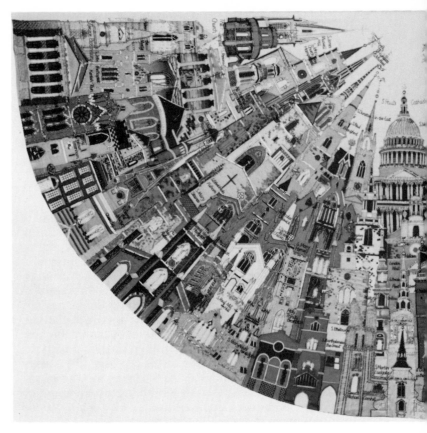

29. *The Silver Jubilee Cope 1977. The conception and design of the project by Beryl Dean. Worked by members of her class at the Stanhope Adult Education Institute and given to the See of London. Generally displayed in the Treasury, St Pauls Cathedral, London. (Photo: Millar & Harris.)*

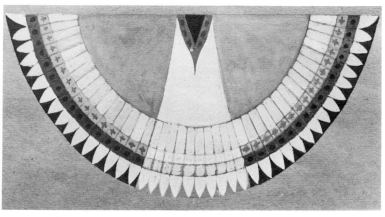

30. *Design for a cope, based upon the Dove symbol, by Jane Lovesy.*

31. Mitre for the Bishop of Ripon. Beryl Dean. Embroidered in gold upon cloth of gold.

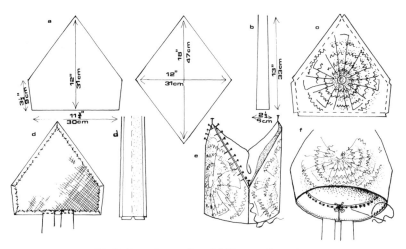

32. Pattern for a mitre. Making up the mitre.

are tacked out on the fabric, and the embroidery completed. It is cut out allowing turnings (32C).

The stiffening can be buckram, sparterie or canvas. The front and back pieces are cut out, minus turnings, these are covered with soft material, such as mull muslin or the cut edges only are covered; if these are stuck, the fabric adhesive should be used very sparingly.

Put the stiffening on the reverse side of the embroidery, fold the turnings over; check to see that the embroidery is not tightly stretched when it is bent round as it would be, when worn. Catch stitch or very lightly stick with suitable adhesive (32d).

Make and attach the lappets, either side of the centre back (32 b–d).

Cut out the lining, allowing turnings, these are folded in, pinned in position and hemmed or slip stitched round the back and front pieces.

Put the sides together and overcast (32e).

Cut out the fabric for the gusset, tack down the turnings (this is unlined). Match up the points of the gusset with the corresponding points of the mitre, pin (32e). Overcast or slip stitch, if this is invisible there is no need to cover with couching or cord.

Procure or make a headband of thin leather, if it has punched holes around the top, a narrow ribbon can be threaded through. If pulled up, the size can be slightly regulated (32f).

If perforations are made with the unthreaded machine needle around the bottom of the headband, it makes the sewing of the leather to the inside of the mitre much easier (32f).

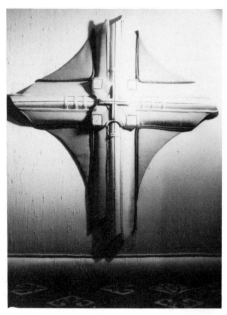

33. *Parts of the Festal and Trinity altar frontals for St Mary of Ottery, Devon. Three-dimensional design worked out by Jennifer Rivett.*

4

Soft Furnishings

Altar Frontals

Through the influence of the Vatican Council the main stream of Liturgical worship, together with the Protestant, Anglican and Episcopal Liturgics has been revised. As a result of this reform churches are discouraged from having a traditionally vested altar with pulpit on one side and lectern on the other. Now, as a part of the process of bringing all the action towards the people the interest is divided between the ministry of the word, the pulpit desk, lectern or ambo with their appropriate falls decorated in the colour of the season – and the ministry of the sacrament served from a free-standing altar without a frontal. The main purpose for this is that the complete front figure of the priest is seen, partly through the altar. The colour of the chasuble forms the background to the action, therefore its length is extended.

The frontal having been dispensed with, there is a subsequent loss of colour, this is compensated by the president's chasuble, the wide stoles of the concelebrates and by the longer and more interesting lectern and other falls.

The Fair Linen Cloth thus gains in importance. In the States great white cloths fall to the ground at both ends of the altar.

Large, seasonally coloured, embroidered falls are laid across the altars of some churches in West Germany.

As an alternative the Laudian or Throw-over frontal is used in many churches. And in the coming years the flat or stretched and mounted frontals may be retained and used upon the redundant high altars, set against the east-end wall, as these frontals may need to be replaced from time to time instructions for their construction are included.

THE LAUDIAN OR THROW-OVER FRONTAL

Because of its size and weight this is a difficult job to tackle and requires both space and skill in the preparation. The textiles selected must not be too heavy.

Storage is an additional problem. At Manchester Cathedral, Judy Barry and Beryl Patten overcame this difficulty by having one off-white Throw-over frontal, on which were fixed three embroidered panels, each set designed in the colour of the season and changed accordingly.

In other churches interchangeable decorative orphreys which

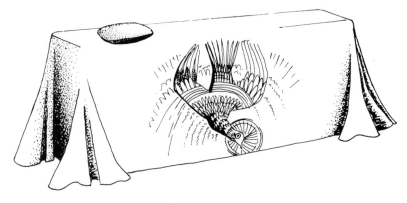

34. Throw-over frontal.

hang down, over the front of the altar frontal (or of the altar itself) are used, when it is impossible to have one for each season. With careful planning it would be possible to make a reversible frontal.

Method of construction: The throw-over or Laudian frontal

If the seams are to run along the length of the altar, it is advisable to arrange for these joins to correspond with the edges of the altar (which means cutting the material to waste, but the pieces can be used for falls, etc.).

This is easier if the seams of the lining (sateen) are in the same position. The amount of material required is three times the length of the altar + twice its height from the ground + twice the width of wide hems.

When the embroidered decoration for the frontal needs to be framed up for working, it is more convenient to arrange to have one central width of fabric measuring from the front across the altar to the back + hems.

When the embroidery has been completed one or more widths of fabric are seamed to each side.

If lack of space makes it necessary, the corners may be rounded. Sometimes a strip of furnishing or pelmet buckram is inserted between the hem (about 9 cm wide) and the reverse side of the fabric.

When making the throw-over or pall frontal with its seams running lengthwise, press open the seams after stitching. Then stitch the seams of the lining and press.

Turn in the hem, about 8 cm, or, if there is to be buckram, about 11 cm wide. Press. Catch stitch if necessary.

Spread out the frontal flatly, face downwards. With the wrong side of the lining to the wrong side of the frontal, spread out the lining, checking to see that the seams are exactly over the seams of the frontal.

Put weights over one half of the lining, and fold it back, down the centre (35), the hem is shown in dotted lines.

Lock the edge of this fold with tiny stitches to the reverse side of the frontal (see 35a, b), starting and finishing some 20 cm from the edges. The stitches are about 6 cm long.

Then move the fold of the lining over until it is on top of the seam, catch the turning of the frontal and of the lining together. Move up the weights.

Make another fold in the lining further on, and stitch that.

Next remove the weights from the other side, fold back that piece of lining and lock the turnings together, continue as before.

Put a tack around the whole rectangle, at about 14 cm in from the edge.

Turn in the lining, arrange the corners, and slip stitch or hem the edge.

For rounded corners cut to shape, turn up the hem, make, press and slip stitch the darts to shape the hem to fit. Then line.

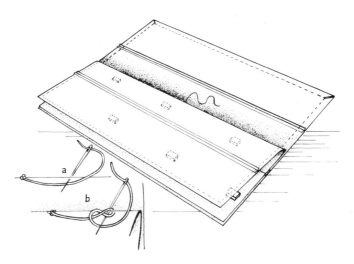

35. Locking the lining to the reverse side of the frontal.

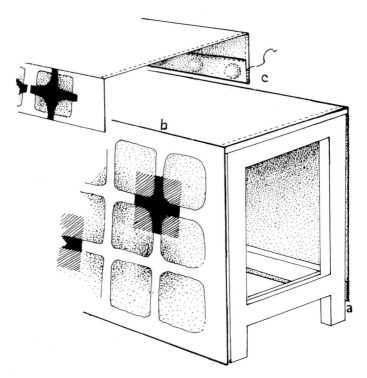

36. Making up an altar frontal.

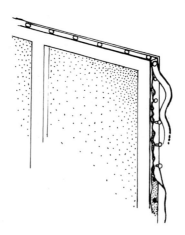

37. Mounting a frontal.

To make up an altar frontal (36)

When the fabric is sufficiently wide the background can be cut with the grain running along the width of the altar, so avoiding joins.

Otherwise make the joins, press open, complete the embroidery. Stretch if necessary.

Put the finished embroidery face down upon a flat surface.

Shrink the interlining. Sail cloth or cotton duck.

Join, and cut to shape.

Put the interlining over the back of the embroidery, matching up the balance marks for the centres.

Fold the edges of the embroidery over the interlining and catch stitch in preference to using adhesive.

To attach the embroidery to the interlining, use a long needle and fine thread, work from the front, take tiny stitches into the outline and very long ones at the back, at intervals along sections of the design, this keeps the two together (it is a good tip to use for very large banners).

Next, spread the lining over the back of the frontal (to catch it to the interlining down the centre prevents it dropping).

Fold in the turnings and slip stitch around three sides, leaving the top open.

For a simple method of suspension, take a length of linen which measures the depth of the altar and about 3/4 of its height. Join to its sides extra widths of fabric to equal the width of the altar frontal.

Stitch narrow hems along the sides, and a wide hem along the bottom (36a).

Then, taking the front cut edge of the linen, put the centre to the centre front of the embroidered frontal.

Slip the edge between the embroidery and the linen (36b).

Slip stitch, using a very strong thread, and hem the lining.

(It is easier, but not so neat, to stitch the four sides of the frontal and press back the front turning of the linen. Then, putting the wrong sides facing, overcast neatly the edges together.)

Insert lead weights and sew up the ends of the hem (36c). Or leave the ends open and push through a heavy rod.

When a super frontal or frontlet is required, it can be made and mounted in the same way (36c).

To the embroiderer the most satisfying method of mounting a frontal is to stretch the embroidery over a wooden stretcher, but this is now seldom used. Unbleached calico covers the stretcher, and is tacked down, over this is stretched the embroidery, the edges are neatened with tape as can be seen in the illustration (37). (The tacks are not hammered home until the whole thing is finally adjusted.)

Pulpit, Lectern, Ambo and Desk Falls

One of the results consequent upon the establishment of the free-standing altar is the gradual disappearance of the altar frontal, and with it goes one source of colour. To compensate there can be more emphasis upon decoration in other parts of the building.

38. *A present day form of Lectern at All Hallows by the Tower, London. Shown also is the cassock-alb with wide stole.*

So the pulpit, lectern, ambo or desk being the other centre of action – the place where the Word is preached – becomes increasingly important. To this end the fall can be made considerably longer, with embroidered decoration planned to make an impact as a focal point.

The designing of a fall makes the same sort of interesting challenge as an altar frontal presents. Basically the main colour is generally but not necessarily, the Liturgical colour of the season.

Hangings are used in other ways to emphasise the Liturgical action, one such example is the fine appliqué panel at the back of the pulpit of Derby Cathedral.

Measurements

The width of the fall is determined by the width of the lectern, desk or ambo, and most are much longer than they were formerly. The bottom can be curved or pointed as an alternative to the rectangle.

Method of making up a fall

Cut a rectangle of fairly heavy interlining, sailcloth, old-fashioned deck-chair canvas or heavy dowlas, but if the thick vilene is used the bottom of the fall needs to be slightly weighted.

Cut, allowing 2 cm turnings around the completed embroidery, and spread it out, face down, upon a table, match up the centres whilst placing the interlining in position on the back. Cut across the corners and arrange the mitres. Fold over the turnings of the sides and the bottom. Attach by catch-stitching or stick with adhesive (39a).

Allowing turnings, cut out the lining, pin in position and fold in the turnings, slip stitch or hem around the three sides of the fall (39b).

Tack across the top of the rectangle.

Sateen is a satisfactory material to use for the lining.

Next, cut two rectangles of strawboard or thin hardboard to fit the top of the desk or lectern.

Cut a rectangle of lining + turnings.

With the two pieces of stiffening in position fold over and stick the turnings, neatening the corners (39c).

Put a piece of elastic across the back of the underpiece of stiffening, stitch or stick the ends (39d). (This is one way of attaching the board to the desk.)

Then, with the two pieces of stiffening together overcast (39d).

Slip the top edge of the fall between the two covered boards and stitch with a strong thread (39e). (A curved needle is an advantage.) See the finished pulpit fall illustrated (41b).

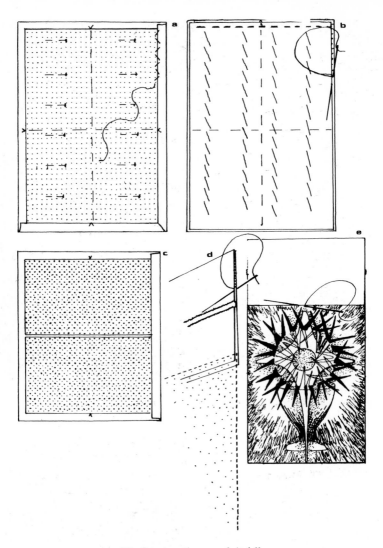

39. *Constructing a pulpit fall.*

Altar antependium, pulpit and lectern falls. Universalist National Memorial Church, Washington, D.C., U.S.A. Designed and made by Conni Eggers.

'Honda' chasuble, synthetic threads, hand couched and designed by Marjorie Coffey (Washington, D.C.) for a National Liturgical conference.

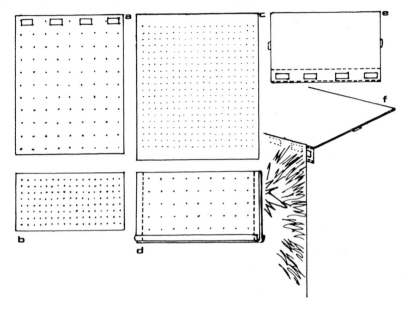

40. *Attaching a fall to the board.*

Method Two

This is a very quick and economical way of attaching several palls to one board.

Make up the fall as before, but neaten the top edge also. Sew about four pieces of Velcro on the wrong side, (40a).

Cut a board to shape (40b).

Cut a rectangle of sateen measuring twice the length of the board + 10 cm, by the width of the board + 4 cm for turnings (40c).

Fold along the centre with right sides facing, and machine stitch each side (40d).

Turn through to the right side. Turn in the bottom edges. Slip the board inside.

Machine stitch across, at the bottom of the board and along the edge of the wide turning.

Sew to this corresponding pieces of Velcro (40e).

Sew a piece of elastic across the width or across the corners. The one board can be used for any number of falls (40f).

41A. Design for Pulpit Fall by Beryl Dean. St Mary, East Guldeford, Sussex.

41B. *Pulpit Fall. Beryl Dean. (To show a fall attached to the board, with the elastic.) St Mary, East Guldeford, Sussex.*

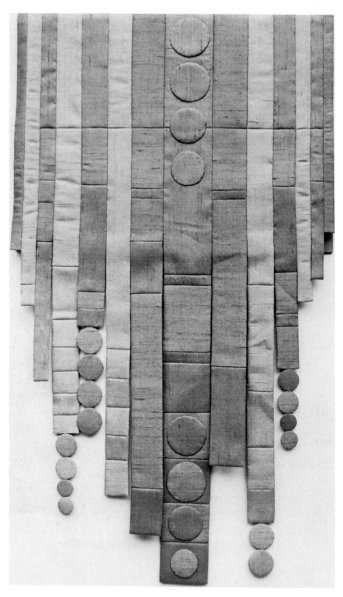

41C. Pulpit Fall. Morna Grafton. (The ends of the drops were weighted with leads.)

42. *Hanging for St Paul's Cathedral, London. Machine embroidery by Pat Russell. (Photo: Keith Ellis* ARPS)

Banners

The designs of banners could, usually, be so much more exciting than they are, when compared to the glowing colours used in the age of chivalry. There is much scope for an original approach to the planning of banners, and the opportunity for creating formalised figures or interesting compositions is limitless, and there is the chance to use fabulous colour combinations and fabrics. For far too long the influence of traditional banners with their sentimental figures and their orphreys has persisted.

Banners and pennants are important today as an additional means of introducing colour into the interior of churches.

Every aspect requires a fresh appraisal; if figure of animal subjects are introduced they should be professionally drawn, nothing is worse than having to look at something which is out of drawing and wrongly constructed, however formalised it may be. The intentionally naïve figure can be delightful but may not be acceptable to the more sophisticated.

The form of the lettering requires equal attention and the most careful draftsmanship. Pat Russell's book on the subject is helpful and her own work a splendid example. Really interesting hand-made fringes make a good finish to the base, but the machine produced fringes are seldom pleasing.

The design of banner poles requires a fresh appraisal as most are so old-fashioned and out of keeping with the present-day idiom. A pole constructed in sections which can be dismantled makes its transportation easier.

Method

The measurements of a banner vary according to the width of the existing pole and the purpose for the banner. It cannot be over long or the vision of the person carrying the banner is obscured, nor should it be too heavy to carry in the wind.

It is essential to work on a table large enough to keep the banner out flatly throughout.

The main part of the banner is made up in the way described for the pulpit fall, except that all four sides are turned over and attached to the interlining (which should have been shrunk). For a large subject it may be necessary to stitch the embroidery to the interlining, this is done by making a tiny stitch on the right side, with a long one on the back of the interlining.

The 4 or 6 loops, called 'sleeves', are made and sewn to the top, where a space must be left in the centre for the pole fitment (43).

The preparation for alternative hem lines for the bottom of the banner are shown at (a) clipping the turning before folding over on to the interlining, and at (b) a curve. Should a fringe be added it is sewn to the back of the banner, to be neatened by the lining.

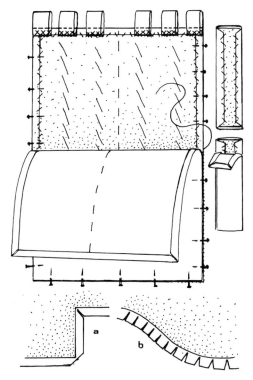

43. Making up a banner.

Taffeta, poult or sateen can be used for the lining which, if it is large, needs to be tie locked to the interlining, this is explained in relation to Laudian or Throw-over frontals.

A loop or tie is sewn on the back, positioned $\frac{2}{3}$ of the way down, this prevents the banner hanging too far away from the pole.

Aumbrey Curtain

If embroidered the curtain is generally rectangular, and is intended to hang with little or no fullness, so its softness is retained by using Jap silk for the lining. To it tiny rings are sewn, or a facing is stitched along the inside of the top edge, and through this a small rod is slotted.

Occasionally an embroidered aumbrey curtain is stiffened in the form of a panel, then rings or hooks are attached to it. The method chosen is the one which is neatest and least clumsy for the individual aumbrey.

The Burse and Veil

The burse and chalice veil are not used in the modern form of celebration. But they are required for the traditional service. The burse is one of the most exciting pieces of embroidery to undertake as there are really no limitations, the Liturgical colours need not be observed, although they are frequently followed.

Many embroiderers fail to consider the purpose of the veil, and make the mistake of using heavy, thick, stiff fabric, or apply thick ornament, even felt! It is essential that the veil should be soft, pliant and light as it covers the chalice when standing on the altar. Any ornamentation is generally in the centre of the front, and it is this side which is folded back when in use.

In the Church of England the burse is usually 23 cm square and the veil 53–61 cm square, the burse is somewhat larger also the veil, when used in the Roman Catholic Church.

Burse boards can be bought either cut in card or plastic, thinner for the front and back lining, these are covered with white linen, the diagram (45A) shows the lacing, it can be stuck but is not so taut. The hinge is made with a narrow strip of linen which is hemmed to the top of both front and back (45B).

One thicker burse board is covered with fabric, this is the back, and there should be a wider turning at the top. The turning at the bottom is stitched through the card, then pinned in position (45C) and the sides of the fabric are laced across from side to side.

44. Burse, veil and stole in green, designed and carried out by Jennie Miskin. (Photo: Studio John Wells.)

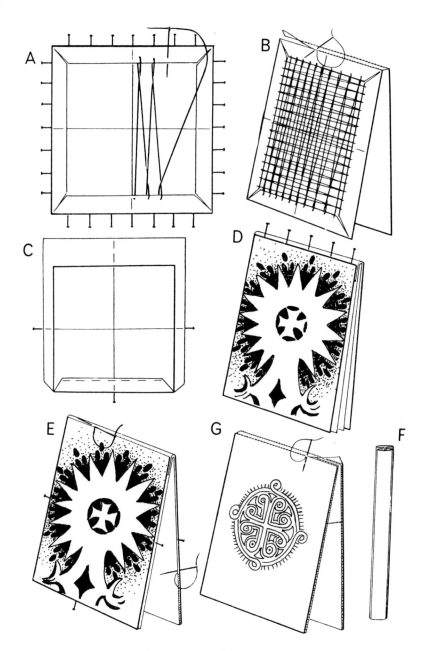

45. Two ways of making up a Burse.

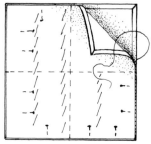

46. Making the chalice veil.

Retain the backing of the embroidery, as this strengthens the work, pin the square over the burse board and lace it across the back or use adhesive.

With the linen-covered boards in place, hold the back board in position with the wide turning at the top, then put the front square with the design standing the right way up, or sideways if the burse is to be used in that way.

Tuck the wide turning down, behind the front square to form a hinge as shown in the diagram (45D).

Slip-stitch invisibly (a curved needle may make this easier) then invisibly slip-stitch or overcast around the edges (45E). Unless a cord is necessary as a means of covering untidy stitching, it is preferable to leave the edges plain. Two little bars are worked across to prevent the corporal from falling out.

In some countries, coloured silk materials are used instead of linen. Alternative methods:

Cover four boards, two with fabric and two with linen, overcast together one from each pair, repeat for the other. Cut and fold the edges of a narrow strip of fabric, measuring, when finished, the width of the burse, line it with linen (45F).

Pin the strip in place to form a hinge at the top edge of the burse as shown (45G). Sometimes this hinge is replaced by four small embroidered bars, worked across from side to side.

A very quick way to make up a burse is to put together the right side of the embroidery and the linen, and to machine stitch round three sides, turn through to the right side, and slip a board into place, the fourth side is slip stitched or overcast, this is repeated for the back, and the hinge made as before.

To make the veil the turnings are folded over and pressed. The edges of the lining square are turned in and pressed. Smoothed out flatly the lining is spread over the back of the work and the edges slip stitched together (46).

Hangings

Made up on the same principles as the banners or throw-over frontal, it is generally unnecessary to add an interlining. But if it is intended that it should fall in folds, a thin interlining, such as mull muslin might be used.

47. *Curtains designed and machine embroidered by Pamela Newton. Tones of blue and yellow. St Nicolas, Chiswick. (Photo: Vic Stedman of Chiswick)*

There are several alternative ways for suspending hangings, curtains or riddles.

To the top can be sewn rings or hooks.

With a false hem (facing) a rod can be pushed through.

On to the top edge of a huge handing made in the U.S.A. they attache- Velcro, and a strip of wood on the wall was similarly covered.

The curtain tape which pulls up is used either when the hanging is to be flat or to fall in folds.

If decorative pleats are to be made, a strip of upholstery buckram is attached between the curtain fabric and lining, to this is sewn the prepared curtain tape.

Only for the traditional English altar is the cord lacing used for hanging the riddles and dossal.

A flat panel might be mounted upon a stretcher.

Alms Bags

With the increase of planned giving the flat pocket form of alms bag is not large enough and is now generally used for smaller services. It adds to the interest when different shapes and decorations are created, provided that they are strong and practical.

Canvas work, because it is so hard-wearing is specially suitable for alms bags, but a very fine canvas should be used, and the stitchery taken up to the fitting line (not over the turnings) otherwise the result is clumsy. Stranded cotton, silk or metal thread can be used as an alternative to wool.

Method
1. Two pieces of outer fabric are cut (plus turnings) for the back part and one of interlining (48a).
2. Cut one pocket piece (embroidered) (b), and one of interlining and another in strong lining material or chamois leather, these are stitched together as shown in the diagram.
3. The pocket area of the inside of the back piece can be made of chamois leather for strength.
4. The completed front and back pieces are put together, and the edges are overcast (c).

It is important to put centre balance marks and to match these up. (The edge can have a cord if necessary.)

This is the basic principle upon which other types of collection bags are constructed.

Planned giving means that larger alms bags are required, the size depending upon the estimated number of envelopes to be collected. Therefore the type of bag attached to a mount is more suitable, but these mounts should be individually designed and made with the collaboration of the woodwork and metal worker,

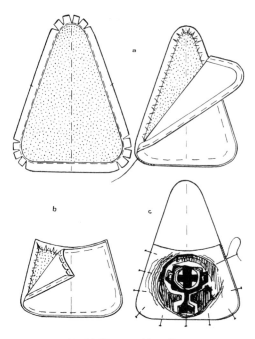

48. Making an Alms Bag.

so that they are interestingly different. Two examples are given.

Fine canvas work, provided that the stitchery does not extend into the turnings, embroidery, upon thin leather or strong fabric, inlay or appliqué in thin leather and any other method which will withstand hard wear, all can be used for the bag.

Some practical way of attaching the bag to a wooden mount has to be found, such as the use of a wood stapler and white glue.

Method

When the embroidery has been completed and stretched. The pattern for the bag has to be made. This must vary according to the mount and type of handles. The following directions are only a guide to planning the shapes. It is advisable to cut out and make up a trial pattern in calico before cutting out the embroidery. Then check that any corrections are amended both in the embroidery and in the marking out of the pattern pieces, cut out the fabric allowing 2–5 cm turnings.

To make the pattern of the bag for mount (49A) first draw the shape (49.1). For this the top half curve is the same measurement as half the curve forming the mouth of the mount. The bottom

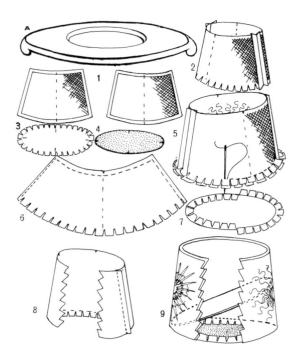

49A. Making up another type of alms bag.

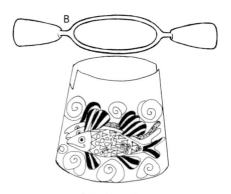

49B. Alms Bag.

curve is parallel with it. Decide the shape and size of the oval base (49.4), half its circumference equals the measurement of the base curve. The depth is decided according to the capacity required, join the sides.

To make the pattern for the lining, these two pattern pieces are put together, seam line over seam line, but slightly overlapped as the lining is always cut slightly smaller.

Cut out the front and back pieces in canvas (or fabric) allowing turnings (49.1).

Seam the sides, (2) and press open.

Cut out the base in strawboard, then cut it in leather or fabric allowing turnings, as at (3). Matching up the centres, attach the base to the side piece as shown at (5) with stab stitching using a very strong thread.

Turn through to the right side, and insert the stiff base, pushing it under the turnings, then stick the turnings to the strawboard.

Place the pattern for the lining upon the chamois or other thin leather (skiver). Allow turnings except on the upper side seam (6).

Cut a slightly smaller oval in card, and in chamois and stick down the turnings (7).

Stitch (or stick) the join of the lining, bend up the turning of the base (8). Insert this lining inside the bag, smooth it out. Stick down the turnings to the base, then put in the stiff lining base (7), right side up. Stick and press it down in place (9).

Bring the seam allowances of the embroidered bag and the lining together at the top and stitch round. It is then attached to the opening in the wooden mount, using the most suitable method. A plastic edging can be used as a neatening.

For a metal mount similar to (49B) the construction of the bag is much the same, except that the outer, embroidered fabric is extended by 4–5 cm at the top, and there should be a gap of at least 1 cm at each side. See the diagram.

These turnings are bent over the metal ring, on both sides, and are hemmed to the top of the lining, on the inside (this is difficult!).

If the fabric used is not stiff, vilene, cut to the size of the pattern (without turnings) can be ironed on to the back of the bag.

Some alms bags of this type are shown in colour.

Altar Cushions

Altar or Missal cushions, when used, measure about 53 cm × 31 cm, but vary greatly. The cushion for the prie-dieu is usually larger.

The textile for the cover selected should not be slippery, nor

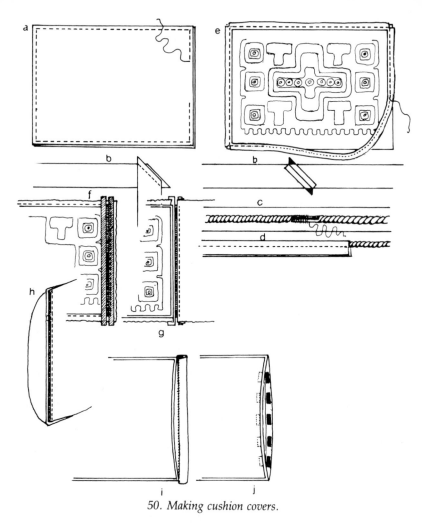

50. *Making cushion covers.*

should any embroidery scratch the binding of the Bible. Generally one cushion is used for all seasons, but detachable covers make for easy changing.

Method

Cut the pillow ticking twice the length by the depth but allow more than 1 cm extra all round + seam allowance on three sides. Leave a section open (50a). Turn through to the right side.

Kapok, if used must be well teased out, or a mixture of horsehair and feathers, if latex foam is used it should be in the form of little cubes, not in one piece (because the book might slide off).

76

The filling is pushed well into the corners, it should be fairly firm but not too full. Some people prefer that a board is inserted to keep it rigid.

To make the cover, cut two rectangles + seam allowance.

If there is to be a piping, cut a strip on the true cross of the fabric which equals the measurement around the cushion + turnings of the join.

Stitch the join and press (50b).

Either cut the piping cord to the exact length or add a little extra, and splice the join (c).

Fold the cross-cut strip over the cord and stitch, using a piping attachment (d).

Pin this piping round one rectangle (e), and stitch.

When it is a permanent cover, the two right sides of the rectangles are put together, and stitched leaving open a gap in one short side, through this the interior of the cushion is pushed, and then it is sewn up.

For a detachable cover sew a dress zip along one short side. After attaching the piping, put the right sides of the zip and the front cushion rectangle together, stitch along this line, using the piping attachment (f).

Fold back the zip, and invisibly catch the turning of the piping and the tape to the wrong side of the fabric, which can be neatened with bias binding.

Next take the rectangle of fabric for the back of the cushion; fold and tack back the turning along one short side. Put this over the zip to hide it. In the diagram at (g) it does not completely cover the zip, whereas in practice it would do so. Stitch, keeping clear of the zip, which is almost closed, and with the right sides of the two pieces of fabric together; stitch round the three remaining sides upon the line of the piping stitching. Open the remainder of the zip and turn through, to the right side.

Alternative method

With the two rectangles together stitch three sides.

Fold back the turning on one side of the front, neaten it by hemming a facing or binding on the reverse side.

Cut a strip which is the length of the short side, and twice the finished width, + turnings, to form a facing.

With the right side of this facing to the right side of the back of the cushion, stitch along the short side. Turn the other edge over to form a lay, and fold it over to the first row of stitches, then hem, as shown at (i).

Tuck in the ends, stitch and fold in this facing. Sew as many pieces of Velcro as required, and sew corresponding pieces on the other side as can be seen in (50j).

Book Covers

Throughout the making of the pattern and the cover the fixing must be done with the book closed.

1. Make a paper pattern to the height of the book, fold this strip of paper round the book, turning in the ends at the front and back covers for about one third of their width. Cut off surplus paper. Mark with little notches the position of these folds and the width of the spine.
2. Choose a fairly thin but firm fabric, not a thick bulky one, unless it is a very large tome.
3. Put the pattern upon the fabric, and tack out the size and mark position of folds and spine. Cut, allowing turnings and a single lay to neaten the folded-back ends.
4. Frame up a thin, firm backing, if it is to be worked this way. Place the fabric on the backing, stitch it in place, transfer the design, work the embroidery. Make sure that the reverse side is as flat as possible. Generally it is better to cut away the backing up close to the embroidery, but if the fabric is limp or rather too thin, the backing may be cut to the exact size of the paper pattern.
5. Invisibly catch down the single lay at the ends (snip away the turning of the lay at the top and bottom to avoid bulk). Then fold over the turnings along the top and bottom, this can be lightly caught down or just pressed.
6. Cut to size a rectangle of very thin material a little less than the width and the height plus turnings. Press down the turnings and lightly hem to the cover, just below the edge, this neatens the inside.
7. Fold this cover round the book when closed. Match up the markings, and fold in the end pieces, then pin (still with the book closed) (51a). Either overcast while still on the book or remove and stitch.

There are other methods and additions to the process which are an advantage when dealing with larger books or missal covers.

An improved fit can be obtained when a little flap of fabric can be left extending above and below the spine (this is finally tucked into the spine). But the bottom of the cut is a problem. Either strengthen the area by ironing-on a small piece of very thin vylene to the reverse side of the fabric (51b), cut and turn back and stitch a tiny turning. Or smear a very little Copydex or other rubber based adhesive (if the material is thick enough for this to be safe). This is to prevent fraying. Then cut down to the tacked

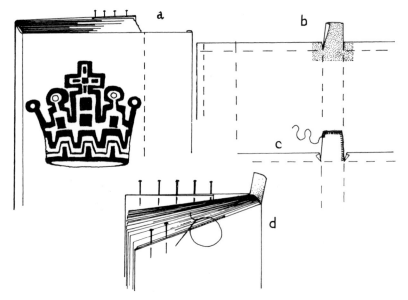

51. Embroidered Book Covers.

line and buttonhole with tiny stitches at the base of the cut and round the edge of the little flap (51c).

A cover will fit better when it is made to be permanent. (And anyway they can be removed by unpicking the top and bottom overcasting at the back of the cover.)

For this, follow the instructions, except that the front and back folds are made three quarters of the width of the book covers. Include the little protruding flaps, but a lining is unnecessary.

Then proceed as before, but overcast only the top and bottom of the front folded-back ends. Insert the front cover into this, tuck the little flaps into the spine, then fold the back of the material round the back cover, and pin, then overcast or slip-stitch the top and bottom whilst in place on the book (51d).

When a thicker material is used for a cover, it is wise to make up the outside only in this fabric, and to take a thinner lining material (the use of the selvedge will make the turned back lay unnecessary) for the inside sections of the fold-over of the covers. Again the front can be hemmed in before putting the cover around the book, and the back can be stitched when in position.

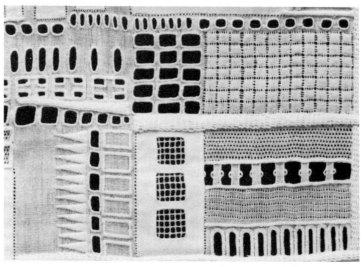

52. Detail of Fair Linen Altar Cloth. Designed and worked by Beryl Dean, 1965. Handwoven linen embroidered in various white-work techniques.

5

Altar Linen

The early fourteenth century embroidered linen altar cloths from Altenberg on the Lahn show a wonderful appreciation of the value of textured patterning carried out in stitchery, and an examination of this use of white upon white is imaginatively stimulating. Large-scale work opens up for us, today, the immense possibilities inherent in linen embroidery.

Linen, decorated with stitchery has been used from very early times, and shows different characteristics according to its origin.

The skilful execution of Victorian fine white-work is unsurpassed (though some was worked in India). It was based almost entirely upon satin stitch, usually raised, and combined with ladder stitch. The designs were generally floral. Ayreshire work has its own characteristics.

During the 1930 era, influenced by Rebecca Crompton, there was an upsurge of interest in discovering new ways of using white and off-white, in which organdie played an important part.

Of particular interest in relation to present-day white-work are some of the methods used in India, for example white cambric applied and finely hemmed to transparent muslin, or the large units composed of shapes filled with different pulled and drawn fillings.

There are many techniques for embroidering upon and with linen threads, these are now being revived and developed in imaginative ways. Traditional methods such as Broderie Anglaise, Richelieu, Hardanger and drawn-thread work form the basis upon which decorative interpretations can be worked out, for this a fresh approach to designing is imperative. For the working upon white (or off-white) linen information is given in the following pages.

When experimenting with embroidery for altar linen it is really important to observe the limitations imposed by the necessity for laundering. Church linen has to withstand frequent washing, and if too many threads are withdrawn the fabric is weakened; the tip of the iron tears holes which are too large, and tassels and fringes are spoilt in a washing machine. These practical considerations do not apply for panels or hangings which can be dry-cleaned.

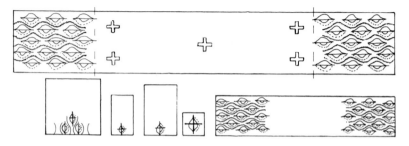

53. *Set of altar linen.*

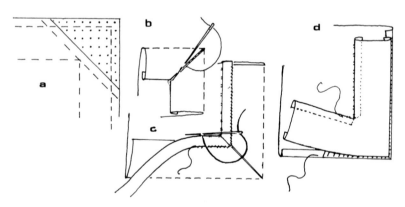

54. *Neatening hems and corners.*

Material

The fabric used for covering the altar must be linen, but it need not necessarily be very fine. The aesthetic value of coarse, textured linen woven with unevenly spun threads is today considered equal to fine machine produced fair linen. An open weave lends itself to interesting pulled and drawn stitch treatments. When an 'off-white' is acceptable it can be embroidered in white or the material can be applied. Conversely, the stitchery can be carried out in washable threads of neutral colours, on the Continent it has long been the practice to use coloured threads.

Stranded and other mercerised cotton threads, linen, mending and lace threads can be used, but silk turns yellow in time.

Altar linen comprises the Fair Linen or Altar Cloth, Corporal, Purificators, Lavabo Towels and the Pall (53). For these the decoration usually matches. The Fair Linen cloth measures the length of the altar plus twice the height of the altar from the floor, adding the width of the hem. The width of the cloth exactly equals the measurement of the altar, plus the long side hems which are narrower.

Free-standing or nave altars are often wider, and the ends almost reach to the floor. The embroidery upon these ends can be really interesting, they are important because there is frequently no frontal. Drawn thread, pulled work, appliqué, both hand and machine, can be seen to advantage.

Five small crosses must be worked in the corners and the centre of the top of the cloth when it is on the altar. This does not apply in the Roman Catholic Church.

It seems unimaginative to have hem-stitched hems all round the cloths. It might be preferable to concentrate the interest at the ends, by working handsome wide borders in, for example, needle weaving; and keeping the long sides plain, this can be achieved by facing the hems on the reverse side with linen tape or bias binding.

A mitred corner is the best way of dealing with the corners of hems. To do this cut across diagonally, allowing a narrow lay (54a). Fold in the lay and turn up the hem, then slip stitch, before invisibly stitching the hem (54b).

To achieve a flat hem which is very suitable for thick fabrics, stitch by hand or machine, a linen tape or bias binding to the edge of the hem. Invisibly catch stitch this to the main fabric (54c).

For thick textured materials, turn in a narrow lay around the outside edge. Cut a shaped facing. Put the right side of the facing to the right side of the cloth, stitch. Turn this over on to the wrong side of the cloth fold in the lay and invisibly stitch to the cloth (54d).

Long, hand-made fringes look superb, but they present problems when laundered.

Throughout the set of altar linen the long sides are generally finished with narrow hems, and good, wide hems at the ends are preferable.

The Credence Cloth is made to fit the measurements of the table, and matches the fair linen in all respects.

THE CORPORAL

The chalice stands upon the corporal in the centre of the altar, for this reason the embroidery must be flat. Open work should be avoided because fragments of the Host might adhere to it. The corporal is considered to be very sacred.

Folded in three both ways, the corporal is kept in the burse, so the embroidery should be planned with this in mind. The hem treatment usually matches the set. The finished square measures 51–56 cm in the Church of England, and slightly larger in the Roman Catholic Church.

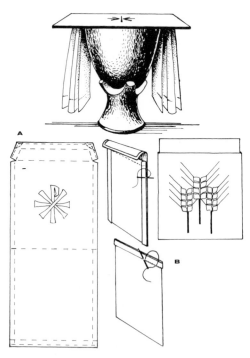

55. Chalice with purificator, paten, pall. Making the pall.

This is used for drying the Holy Vessels during the Celebration, the purificators vary in size, but usually measure 23–31 cm by 31–36 cm or sometimes square. The Purificators used in the Roman Catholic Church are rather larger rectangles. Folded in three lengthwise, there can be a small embroidered symbolic motif.

LAVABO TOWELS
Used by the priest before the Consecration, the size varies, but is generally about 61 by 31 cm or less, but slightly smaller when used in the Roman Catholic Church. These towels are folded in three lengthwise and may be embroidered with a small motif.

THE PALL
When dressing the chalice, the folded purificator is first placed across the chalice; and over this the paten (which in the diagram does not show) with the priest's wafer upon it; this is covered by the pall which is a stiffened square (55). (Sometimes a second corporal is used instead, which is folded in three both ways to form a pall, a small cross is embroidered in the centre, and is folded with this uppermost.) The pall is used in the Roman Catholic Church but not always in the Church of England.

Made of fine linen the pall usually measures about 15 cm square. The embroidered design, which is arranged centrally, is generally based upon a cross.

The square of stiffening can be plastic, perspex or card.

One method of making up is on the principle of an envelope (55).

Tack out the shape, complete and press the embroidery.

Cut out, adding turnings and a lay at one end, and shape the other end, allowing turnings, to from the flap, as in the diagram (A).

At the other end hem or hemstitch. Turn down the hems.

Cut across the corners of the flap, fold the turnings, arrange the mitres, tack, hem and press.

Fold the side turning, and with right sides together, overcast, as shown in the diagram.

Turn through to the outside and slip the stiffening in place.

At (55B) a simpler method is illustrated, prepare as before, omitting the flap. Make a hem around the opening and invisibly stitch. At (B) the stiffening is shown, it protrudes slightly.

Alternatively the pall can be formed with two squares their turnings folded back, with the wrong sides together, three of the sides are overcast, then the stiffening is put inside and the fourth side is then overcast. When laundered it may be necessary to unpick and re-sew one side, in order to remove the stiffening.

THE AMICE

Worn with the set of traditional Eucharistic vestments, the amice is not required when the cassock-alb and wide stole, or chasuble are worn.

This neck cloth of linen is a rectangle measuring about 63 cm by 91 cm and has a narrow hem on all sides. Two tapes about 1.52 m long are attached at the ends of one long side of the armice.

The apparel measures about 8 cm by 56 cm. After the completion of the embroidery, it is cut out, allowing turnings. A strip of interlining of the exact size is pinned to the back of the embroidery, and the turnings are folded over and catch stitched (or stuck), it is then lined. The apparel is tacked to the amice, and removed when laundered.

SURPLICE COTTA (56)

In the Roman Catholic Church the cotta has, to a great extent, been replaced by this surplice. But when used as a cotta it is short, and as a surplice it is cut longer – to the required measurement.

As the drawn thread borders are distinctive the material must be suitable for this type of embroidery, linen, moygashel or other similar fabrics can be used. This limitation does not relate to other types of decoration.

Having cut out and seamed up the sleeve and skirt pieces, mark out the hem width and withdraw the threads in preparation for the drawn-thread work borders, some examples are shown (at diagram 62). Hem-stitch the hems.

Making up

Taking an average measurement for the chest and back width, make a pattern for the yoke, cut two of each in fabric.

Stitch the shoulder seams of each, then putting the right sides of the yokes together, stitch round the neck. Turn through, and on the right side stitch again round the neckline. Mark a line for the turnings around both the yoke and the lining.

Shape the top of the sleeve, and the armholes of the skirt pieces, checking that the measurement of each fit.

Arrange the pleats on each side of the centre of the front and back to correspond to the yoke measurements, and allowing for the armholes.

Put the centre of the right side of the skirt to the centre of the right side of the yoke, arrange the pleats, tack and stitch. Another row of stitching on the right side will keep the pleats flatter.

Repeat for the back. While this is being done, pin back the lining yoke, out of the way.

Next, fix the sleeves in position, with the right side of the sleeve to the right side of the yoke, stitch and press.

Then fold in, and tack the turnings of the yoke lining, and place this over the reverse side of the completed garment. Hem by hand. This neatens the joining of the pleats and sleeve tops.

If the armholes and the underarm of the sleeves are stitched and neatened at this stage, any adjustment to the fitting can be made.

There are many other ways in which the surplice cotta can be made up. The embroidery can be done before the seams are stitched, if preferred, but this results in a more bulky join.

56. Surplice Cotta.

57. Chalice Veil. Gertie Wandel, Kunstindustrinuscet, Copenhagen.

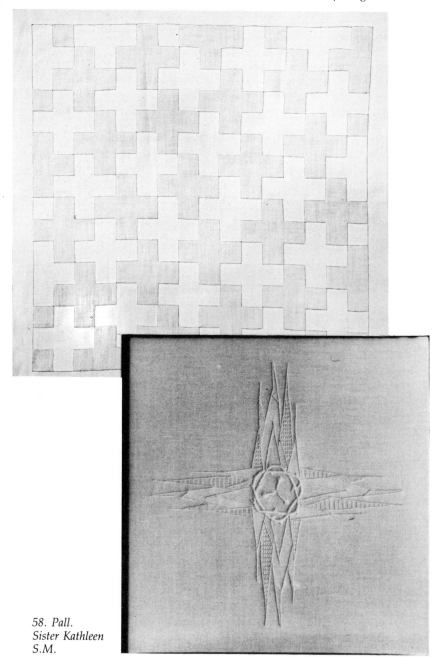

58. Pall.
Sister Kathleen
S.M.

59. *Altar Cloth for the High Altar. Design and embroidery by Liz Wilson and Audrey Bennett. Stitched lines appliqué and embroidery. Shades of red and maroon with bright gold linen appliqué. Derby Cathedral.*

Hand-worked linen embroidery methods

Broderie Anglaise

The characteristic of this method is that the pattern is cut away. Therefore the material should be closely woven to avoid fraying.

To work, outline the individual unit with small running stitches (60a). Then cut into the corners, and, using the needle to fold back a section at a time (b), and overcast the edge (c), with tiny stitches.

The design for Broderie Anglaise (60) could be used in several ways. For example, repeated four times, side by side, a striking border for a fair linen cloth would be achieved. The central portion might decorate items of the remainder of the set. Alternatively, put in the centre of the overhanging end of the altar cloth, this design could be developed with concentric circles of stitchery. This idea emphasises the importance of repeating small units so that they add up to one bold statement.

Traditional Broderie Anglaise is composed of eyelet holes, these are whip-stitched over a foundation of running stitches which continue round half of the hole then on to the neat, returning in a figure eight. The larger holes are cut in the form of a cross and the smaller made with a stiletto.

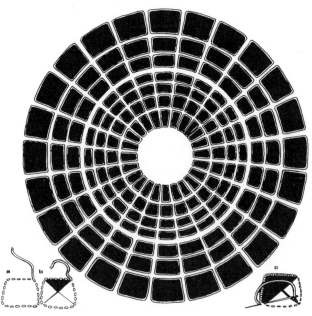

60. Broderie Anglaise.

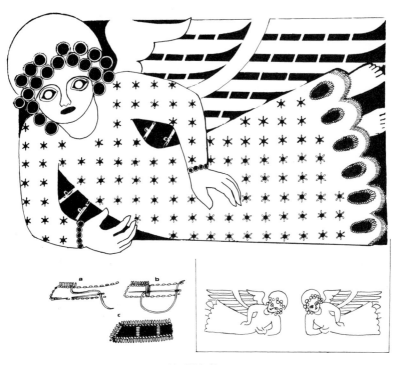

61. *Richelieu.*

Richelieu

It is characteristic of Richelieu that the background of the embroidered design is cut away. It is important to avoid making the holes too large for washing and ironing; this difficulty can be overcome by working decorative bars across the space to add strength (61). Sometimes a picot is worked upon the bar.

Method: Work small running stitches around the outline, then over this do buttonhole stitching, with the heading facing towards the edge to be cut away (a). When a bar is to be included, the buttonhole stitches are worked as far as the position of the bar, then take a stitch across to the other side, and return (b). Take the thread across again, and whip or buttonhole stitch over these three threads to form a bar, then continue to buttonhole edge. When complete the background material is cut away (c).

This is the traditional approach, but with imagination all sorts of exciting variants can be thought up.

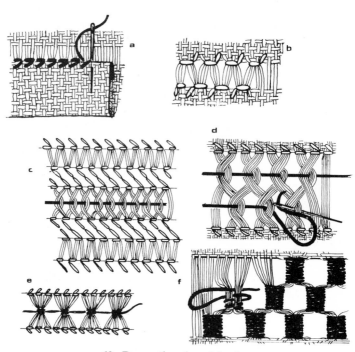

62. *Drawn thread work borders.*

Drawn-thread borders

For a handkerchief-hemstitched hem withdraw two threads, fold the hem, and tack. The stitching is worked on the wrong side, and started with a short length of thread which is worked over as the stitching proceeds from left to right (62a). When more threads are withdrawn both sides are worked. At (b), four threads are taken up, and on the other side two threads from each of two groups are stitched over.

Various open work stitches can be combined to make wide borders (62c), is composed of two lines of split group, the hemstitching has been worked on the right side, is stitched over three threads of the fabric. For the centre border, divide the vertical threads equally. Insert the needle from right to left under the threads of the second cluster, next bring the eye of the needle back from right to left, pick up the second half of the first cluster of threads, which is then passed under and in front of the threads of the first group. This is shown at (d) and is known as crossing the threads twice and can be followed from the diagram.

Faggot open work is worked over a foundation of groups of two threads. Then, having secured the working thread, make

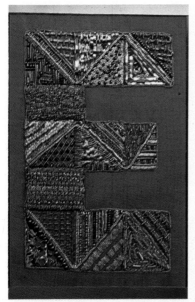

Experimenting with gold threads, Angela Schmidt and Daphne Wells, London College of Fashion.

Design based on pomegranate tree shows Irish, Cornely and Bernina machine embroidery. By Judy Barry and Beryl Patten, Chester Cathedral.

Alms Bags, in canvas work, by the embroidery group of St Michaels, Highgate, London.

'The Heart' Pulpit Fall, Hannah Frew Patterson.

three back stitches around every three clusters. At the third stitch, slip the needle under the first two to fix the thread, the working thread should not be pulled up too tightly. This can be followed at (e) in the diagram.

Many patterns can be devised by using darning, it will be seen at (f) that it is unnecessary to hemstitch the edges.

Pulled and drawn thread-work

For pulled-work fillings a fairly loosely woven linen is necessary and a fine thread is usually used. There are many decorative stitches, a few are given in the diagram (63).

(63a) is wave filling; it will be seen that the needle passes behind four threads and over four threads, then it is taken down between two threads of the previous group of four threads and is brought up on the other side of two threads of the next group.

Rows of ridged and open work stripes are effective, when worked as a pulled stitch, as shown at the reverse side at (b). The double-back stitch is worked over about six or eight horizontal threads, picking up four threads above and splitting the group below. This is repeated for the next row, when the same four threads of linen are picked up. The right side is illustrated on the right.

For a closely woven material two or more threads are withdrawn, the double-back stitch is pulled fairly lightly to form ridges, the finished effect is shown.

For drawn-thread work the threads of the fabric are actually withdrawn, so the outline must first be worked, generally over a small running stitch, over which buttonhole or trailing (63a) is stitched.

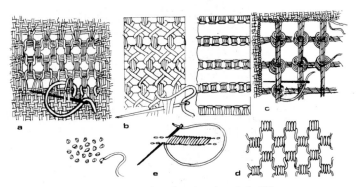

63. Pulled, drawn thread and satin stitch fillings.

At (63c) four threads are withdrawn and four remain in each direction. These are whipped in both directions with a very fine thread. For this attractive pattern little wheels are darned around the intersections of the threads, if worked on the reverse side, the working thread can be passed to the next one quite invisibly. It is possible to work this on a large scale with thick threads, varying the sizes.

(d) is one of the many counted thread patterns worked in satin stitches on the right side of the material. But in this example the needle passes behind one group of stitches, then goes through those of the group below. A fairly coarse sewing cotton enhances the effect when used for this last stage in the execution.

(e) Slanting satin stitch is generally worked over small running stitches, or to obtain a raised effect, over a padding of stem stitches.

(f) Seeding gives an irregular texture, a small back-stitch is worked, and over this another. Or the larger stitches are worked at random.

Trailing (64a) makes a useful outline, but it should be worked in a frame. Tiny overcast stitches are worked over a padding composed of a bunch of three thicker threads at the beginning and ending of these threads they are taken through to the wrong side and cut off.

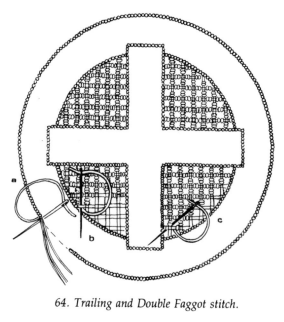

64. *Trailing and Double Faggot stitch.*

65. Free smocking, white on white. Jean Curran.

Double Faggot stitch (64b and c) can be worked as a pulled stitch or as a drawn thread stitch, according to the scale of the work. It is worked diagonally on the right side of the fabric, first the vertical threads are whipped with two stitches then the needle passes diagonally behind and the horizontal threads are whipped (b), the needle again passes behind the intersection of the threads (c).

To work the entire background with pulled or drawn thread work, throws the design into relief, and creates a large scale composition of shapes which is very suitable for church linen. Conversely the design can be carried out in Eye or Algerian Eye stitch.

Appliqué is generally attached with Pin-stitching which is worked from right to left (66), the edges of the piece to be applied are turned under and it is tacked to the background. The pin stitching is worked with a very fine thread and coarse needle, on the right side of the piece of work.

When the design is applied in an opaque linen upon a slightly transparent linen, a most satisfactory effect is produced. But the areas should not be too large as they do not launder well.

The drawing (67) shows a detail from an experimental example of white-work demonstrating textures obtained by combining various traditional methods and stitches worked on a loosely woven background. Such embroidery would have to be pinned out after washing, whilst still wet, over blanket and clean cloths, wrong side uppermost. Then with a dry cloth over, it would be dried off with a hot iron.

These examples (67, 68) which demonstrate a present-day approach would lend themselves excellently as bold, attractive decoration for altar cloths, it is an imaginative way of using traditional methods which combine well with a wooden or stone altar. But the people who have the enjoyment of creating these delightful articles seldom have to cope with the ironing!

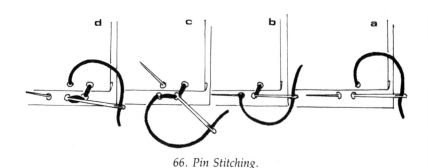

66. *Pin Stitching.*

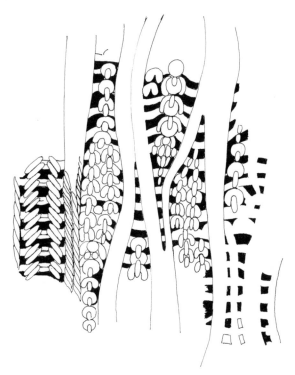

67. Various stitches worked with a thick thread upon an open weave. Experimental darning and needle weaving on loosely woven curtain fabric, using ribbons also smooth, matt and textured threads.

It will be seen from the illustrations that many embroidery stitches can be used for the decoration of altar linen, for example, many rows of stem-stitch worked with a narrow space between, or simple blanket stitch, pointing outwards, worked next to a row of stem-stitch, and repeated, produces a delightful filling. The contrast of both texture and thickness of thread can give quite different appearances to the most ordinary stitches, for example feather stitch in fine sewing cotton put alongside a fine cotton piping cord (washed to shrink it) which has been machine stitched in place.

In the section on Machine embroidery, other ways of dealing with the decoration of altar linen are to be found.

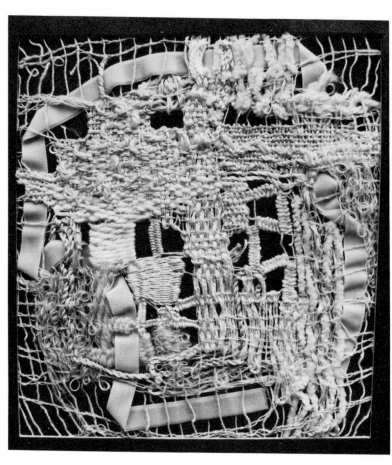

68. Experimenting with textiles. Sheila Kinross.

6

Transferring the Design to the fabric

For much church embroidery accuracy is necessary, so the choice of the method used for transferring the design is important. This is usually done when the material has been framed up, but for very large pieces it has to be done when stretched out flatly on a table, kept in place with weights. The pricking and pouncing method gives the greatest degree of accuracy.

1. Trace the outline of the design upon stout tracing paper.
2. Perforate the outline by pricking holes closely together (69.1), using a fine needle (No. 9), which can be set into a pin vice or a little holder can be made by folding a small square of paper (69.1). It really makes no difference to the result whether this is done from the top or the underside of the tracing paper.
   A thin pad of felt or folded cloth or rubber is put underneath.
3. Put the perforated tracing upon the material, matching up the centre marks. Keep it in place with weights.
4. Make a pouncer by rolling up a strip of felt. Dip this into the pounce, being careful to use it sparingly (69.2).
5. Black pounce is bought as powdered charcoal, and white, when it can be procured, is powdered cuttle fish. As a substitute French chalk can be used.
6. With a little pounce on the end of the pouncer, rub it through the perforations (69.2).

 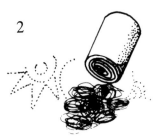

69. 1. Perforating the tracing with a fine needle in a holder made with folded paper. 2. Rubbing in the pounce with a felt pouncer.

7. When complete, carefully lift the tracing away. Then, using a very fine brush and water colour (poster) paint over the outline formed by the little dots of pounce. (When it is certain that there will be no dampness, it can be outlined with a fine felt tip pen, ball Pentell, etc., which is quicker and gives a finer line. But it spreads alarmingly if it comes in contact with dampness.)

8. When complete, flick away the surplus pounce.

Any of the other methods for transferring can be used, such as pinning templates in the required positions and tacking around the outline. Or the pounced outline can be sprayed with a proved fabric fixative spray. This is not recommended for the more precious materials used for ecclesiastical work.

Framing up for hand embroidery

For church embroidery a frame is essential, mainly because work generally is large, and many churches are damp, and this causes embroidery to pucker. The great advantage of using a frame is to keep the work taut and perfectly flat during the process of working.

Framed-up embroidery allows freedom of movement for the hands, so that metal and other threads can be manipulated and intricate stitches executed.

Some stitches are essentially hand stitches, just as techniques such as patchwork gain nothing from being framed-up.

Rectangular slate frames, two rollers and two side bars with four pegs or split pins are recommended for church work, because they can be adapted to various areas of fabric and longer lengths of material can be rolled around the rollers.

The size of the frame is determined by the length of the webbing.

(70A) shows a small frame dressed for a piece of work such as a burse.

1. The sides of the piece of linen or calico backing are folded over string and run stitched with some backstitches, for strength, as shown at (B).
2. At the top and bottom turn down a narrow turning.
3. Match up the centres to the centres of the webbing.
4. Pin the edges together and overcast.
5. Slip the two side pieces or slats through the slots in the rollers of the frame.
6. Extend so that the backing is almost taut, insert the split pins. Check that the measurement of two sides is the same.
7. With string of sufficient length, thread a packing needle, then lace through the sides of the backing and over the side pieces as shown in the diagram (70A). (When some of the

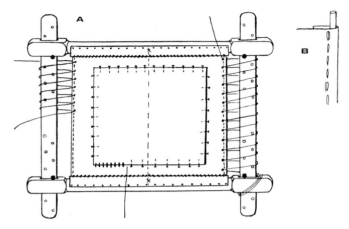

70. Dressing a slate frame.

fabric is wound round the rollers, allow extra string for the
extension.)
8. Cut, to the thread the piece of material to be embroidered
(selvedge running down), tack down the centre.
9. Put this fabric, centre to centre, upon the backing, pin and
stitch, pulling it taut, as shown at (70A).
10. When complete, tighten up the frame.

For large long pieces, which cannot easily be reached, the centre
is first worked then the extra fabric is unrolled.

For domestic and most other embroidery the material can
simply be pinned to square or picture frames, but for this more
specialised work, as the size needs adjusting and the tension
altered, slate frames are recommended.

The vestments and furnishings undertaken for the church are
usually large, and often the embroidery is in the centre, surrounded by fabric on all sides. This presents a problem when
framing-up, apart from the fact that a sufficiently large frame may
not be available, it might be impossible to reach the working area.

To cope with this difficulty, procure a frame large enough to
take the area to be embroidered.
1. Frame up a piece of backing large enough for this area, roll in
any extra width, leaving exposed a size which can be reached.
2. Take the whole piece of fabric. Place the part to be embroidered over the backing, with the surrounding fabric hanging
down on all sides. Match up the centres, smooth out the
fabric.

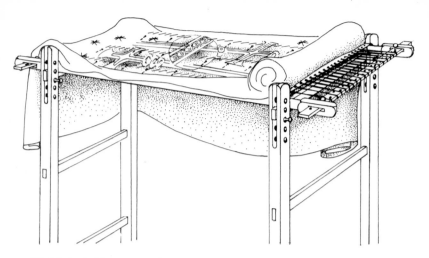

71. Method of framing-up for embroidery upon an area of fabric too large for the frame.

3. Pin in place, keeping the pins all in one direction, then zig-zag tack in lines, this can be seen in the diagram (71) where the frame is shown supported on wooden trestles.
4. Tighten up the frame.
5. The design can be traced on at this stage if it has not been done previously. (Make the surface firm by building it up underneath with books.)
6. Take something soft, such as tissue paper and fold the surplus surrounding material over it.
   Roll up the ends.
   Try not to lean on the folded parts whilst working, because deep creases will not always come out subsequently.
7. When the central section has been completed, unroll the frame to extend it (longer side slats can be made very easily), replace these side arms, lace up the extended area and smooth out the fabric, pin, zig-zag tack, tighten up and complete the embroidery.

   For working small motifs which are powdered over the surface, an easy method for framing up is to use a table clamp tambour frame or a small slate frame.

Take a piece of backing and stitch it into the frame, over it put the small area to be embroidered, fold in the surrounding fabric, complete the embroidery, and cut away the backing, up close to the motif, repeat for each one.

For another more economical method, use either type of frame, or a larger one, take a piece of firm linen or holland of the required size, cut out a hole which is slightly larger than the area to be embroidered. Strengthen the edge with buttonhole stitching or machine stitching. Frame up.

Place the whole area of fabric over the frame, arranging that the motif to be embroidered covers the hole which has been cut out of the linen (or holland).

Smooth the material to be embroidered downwards and across and pin it to the backing linen so that it is taut, for this use needles, as they mark the fabric less, and tack with silk for the same reason.

When the embroidery is complete, the tacks are taken out, the fabric is removed, and the process is repeated for the next motif.

In this age of creative embroidery it is seldom that the method of working the units of embroidery separately upon linen is used. When complete they were cut out and applied to the framed-up background, with the addition of corded outlines and stitched details.

72. *Experiments in creative design to be carried out with metal threads, etc. Jane Pemberton.*

7

Embroidery Methods

Using Metal Threads

The decoration of textiles for the church has, until the present time, been synonymous with couched gold and silver embroidery. Now these traditional techniques are being adapted to the substitute synthetic, plastic and other types of thread. All sorts of new and exciting ways of using this vast variety of threads and braids is being discovered.

These interesting experiments with methods and combinations of threads can only be incorporated into the decoration of vestments and soft furnishings for the church, when they are judged to pass the test of practicability and suitability for purpose. In this respect it is important to find out how much wear and tear the embroidery will have to withstand, for example the chasuble or frontal will be rubbed, therefore it is impracticable to work with loosely spun wool or 'lumpy' raw silk; to find out how the objects will be stored, and how they will be lit are other factors to be borne in mind. Practical limitations have to be observed when designing and creating in any medium.

BASIC METAL THREADS

Japanese Gold and Silver, unobtainable.

Jap. Gold substitute, 20 yd. reels. 1 K thickest – 2, 3 and 4 finest. Lurex cords and twists, 6 m lengths or by the metre.

Lurex cord (flat – hollow) 6 m lengths and Russia braid.

Check (crinkled thread) gold or silver by the metre.

Antique cord (dark) twisted, by the metre.

Cordonnet, variously coloured, fine metallic threads, by the skein from some suppliers.

Bourdon and Guipé (a rough texture, gold, silver) from some suppliers.

Salisbury cord, silk, various colours, plain or twisted with Lurex, by the metre.

Note case cord (thicker) various colours, by the metre.

In the past Japanese gold and silver was the basis of church embroidery, it was made from paper covered with gold leaf which was twisted round a core of pure silk or cotton, and was obtainable in several thicknesses, it was traditionally couched down double, with Maltese, couching or horsetail silk, unfortunately the substitute, New Maltese silk, is very fine. The synthetic Japanese gold is sold in several thicknesses by the reel. Though somewhat 'brassy' in colour, it is pliant and pleasant to work with, but the perfect couching thread is now impossible to find though nylon invisible thread has some advantages when used for this purpose, and spools of Perivale or Perfection silk are produced in good colours.

The following illustrations show the traditional method of couching pure and imitation Japanese gold and some variations (73).

1. The gold is laid upon the surface, and the couching stitch crosses at right angles, they are bricked with those of the previous row. When working a block of solid gold, it is turning at the beginning and end of each row which should not be clumsy. For the method shown at (73.1) a single thread is put down to start, this is then paired with another which is turned round when the end of this row is reached and another new single thread is introduced, this can be followed from the diagram.

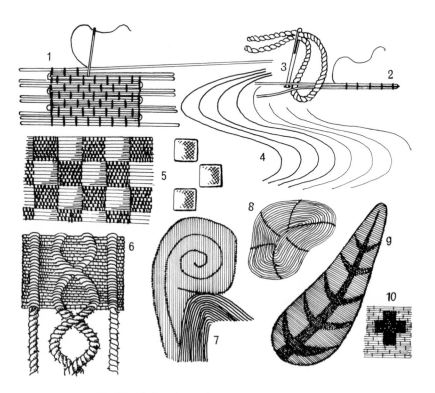

73. Metal threads couched down in various ways.

2. To start a doubled row of gold, first stitch into the loop, then over the two together.
3. The ends of all metal threads are taken through to the reverse side with a sling (a double thread in a chenille needle) (73), these ends are stuck down at the back. For tubular braids, flat braids, etc., a tiny slit or a hole is made in the fabric before pulling the end through, both at the beginning and at the finish.
4. A rhythmical linear effect can be produced by couching down a single thread invisibly. Alternatively repeated lines of gold couched down leaving a space between each is attractive.
5. Raised patterns are made by cutting small shapes in felt, these are stitched or lightly stuck to the background single or double thickness, the first smaller than the final one. The rows of gold are laid over the padded shapes between which they are stitched down.
6. In the past intricate patterns have been achieved by sewing down string or piping cord, over this is couched the metal thread.
7. Single vertical or horizontal threads having been laid upon the background, the sewing-down stitches follow the design traced on the fabric.
8. This example shows a single (or double) thread which follows round the outline of the shape which is gradually filled up, again the couching stitches catch down the metal threads in a pattern.

   This method of filling shapes is deceptively simple, because towards the centre, the shape remaining to be filled can be impossibly difficult to deal with.
9. For more intricate shapes it may be more satisfactory to follow a direction across or downwards, here the veining is stitched in coloured silk.
10. The double rows of gold are sewn with self colour upon the background and the little cross is carried out in colour sewing.

Obviously there are many alternatives, and totally different effects can be produced with the use of any of the many threads and braids, etc. The inventive craftswoman will see the possibilities inherent in couching synthetic threads, a bunch of fine wools, yarns, cotton, string or metallic elastic, etc., they contrast well with rough, smooth or flat strips, this is illustrated at (74).

Basket stitch is a method which is typical of metal thread embroidery because it catches the light, and so gives a rich effect, for this reason it was widely used in the past, and can be adapted

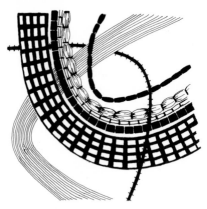

74. Couching in various ways.

to present-day interpretation with the introduction of different textures.

For the foundation rows of string are sewn down, these are spaced according to the thickness of the metal thread, cord, etc. The ends are cut with strong sharp scissors, and are sewn over to prevent fraying, see (75.1).

Traditionally this stitch was usually carried out in Japanese gold, passing thread, plate or stout floss silk. The thread passes over the required number of rows of string, and is sewn down, between two rows, with a strong waxed thread as shown at (75.2). (A dark sewing thread is more effective.) Until the technique has been mastered, it may be helpful to make a little backstitch to fasten tightly the sewing-down thread, this is covered by the gold. The ends are taken through with a sling. But where there is an intricate outline it is advisable to take each thread down separately, as at (3). Here a double thread passes over four rows of string, whereas at (4), a single, thick thread is used, which can be turned at the ends.

A single thread passes over two rows of finer string at (5), and this is repeated. There are many variations of the diagonal line, one of which is shown at (6), this too is over a foundation of finer string.

Many exciting effects can be produced by using experimental threads such as synthetic raffia, thin leather or gold kid thongs, gold plate, guipé or narrow velvet ribbon combined with flat metal threads (76). It may be found necessary to space the rows of string further apart.

The outline edges often require some form of neatening which is in keeping with the design, cords sewn down or a bunch of couched threads are the most useful.

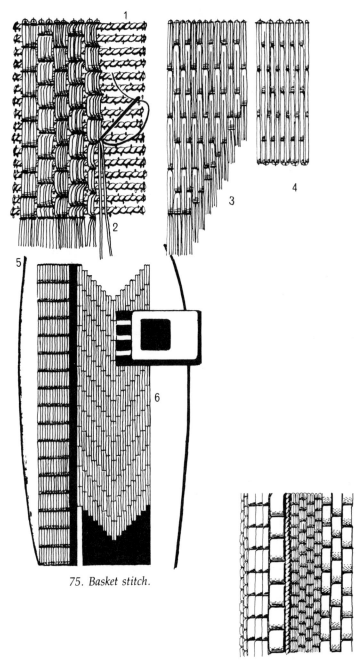

75. *Basket stitch.*

76. *Using leather thongs, ribbon, etc.*

77. Variants of Burden stitch.

Burden Stitch

Parallel rows of horizontal or vertical metal threads (or silk) form the foundation for burden stitch. When the metal thread is one which will thread into the needle, such a passing or tambour, the rows can be laid in the way shown at (77.1). The silk stitches are bricked, and spaced to allow the metal to glint through (77.2). Interesting colour effects are possible. Alternatively, upon a coloured silk foundation, short lengths of gold or silver purl can be stitched as illustrated at (3).

Padding

To raise from the background a shape which is to be covered with gold will add to its richness by catching the light. A three-dimensional effect is popular at the present time, particularly in conjunction with metal threads. For this padding, layers of felt are satisfactorily used. The first layer is small, and the subsequent layers increase in size until the last, which can be cut to the actual shape (if a complicated outline, rub pounce through the pricking). Each is sewn in position (78.1), the final layer requires more stitching (2). For certain methods of work it is sufficient to stick the felt in place.

(78.3). Another way to raise stitchery from the background is to cut out the shape (a fraction smaller) in card, this is sewn to the background. Passing or another suitable thread is crossed over the card from side to side, and at each turn is sewn down.

(78.4). Bright check purl chips are sewn at random using a waxed thread. There may or may not be a padding.

(78.5). To sew cords, the stitches slant with the twist and alternate on either side of the cord. About 2 cm is left at the beginning and end, this is unravelled and pulled through a small hole made with a stiletto, the use of a chenille needle and sling makes this easier. On the reverse side the ends are flattened and stuck back.

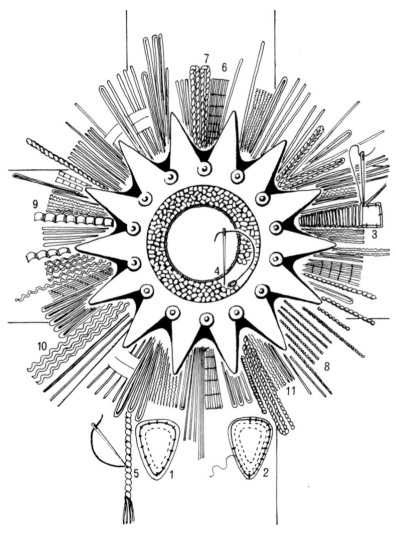

78. *Sewing gold threads and padding.*

79. Processional cross adapted
as a free-standing altar cross
(opposite page). Created and
embroidered by Jean Panter.
For the Parish Church of St
Anne, Highgate, London.

112

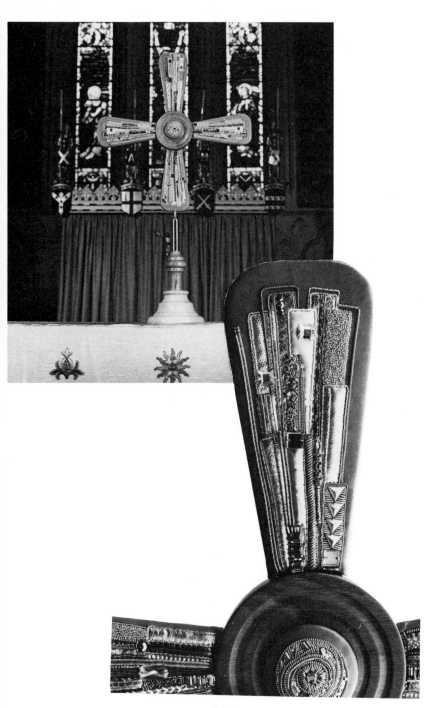

(78.*6*). Long laid stitches, close together, are made with passing or tambour thread, sewn down to form horizontal or diagonal lines.

(78.7). Fine twisted cord, sewn with invisible thread using slanting stitches.

(78.*8*). Super fine Pearl purl sewn in spaced lines, interesting textures can be produced by sewing several rows close together or by alternating these with round smooth threads.

(78.9). Plate, crinkled by holding it over a screw (or comb) indenting it with the fingernail at intervals, the sewing down stitches are taken across the plate and correspond with the indentations.

(78.*10*). These threads are variously called check or large rococo, invisible thread is useful for the stitching. The ends are taken through.

(78.*11*). Groups of fine or thicker twists, contrasted textured threads.

Passing thread is composed of a core of silk, nylon or cotton round which a very narrow strip of metal (gold, aluminium or silver gilt) is twisted. Tambour thread is similar but finer, both can be threaded into the needle, provided that the metal is untwisted for about 2 inches so that only the core passes through the eye of the needle. Most decorative stitches can be carried out using these threads.

Rough, smooth and bright check purl in gold or silver. These very pliant purls are sold by the dram, and are made in three qualities and several sizes, a fine one is No. 8 and the largest are called bullion.

These purls are spun on the principle of a very fine spring, and are cut into short lengths as required, sewn in the same way as for beads, the smallest lengths are called chips (78.4), this makes a fascinating texture when check purl is used. These lengths can be cut more easily if a small board, covered with felt is used, against which the pieces are cut.

Rough purl has a dull gold finish and smooth purl is shiny and smooth. Whereas bright purl is textured and sparkles.

Pearl purl or bead purl is a heavier wire coil, less pliant; it is available in several sizes, the finest being 'superfine'. These purls are used for outlining as they can be manipulated easily, all the different sizes are used in badge-work particularly. These Pearl purls have to be pulled to extend their length, before working, as this enables the sewing-down thread to slip down between the twists.

(80A) Plate, which is taken backwards and forwards across a padding of card, it is sewn at each bend. At the beginning and

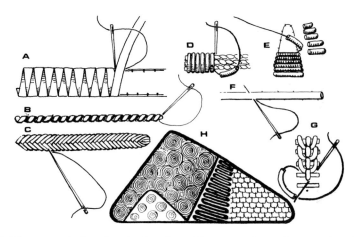

80. How to manipulate the wire threads, and how to sew down plate, rough purl, bead or pearl purl, etc.

ending the plate is cut and folded into a little hook, which is stitched, as can be seen in the diagram.

(80B) Pearl purl, enlarged to show how the stitch crosses between the twists, as the purl has been pulled out. The ends are cut to form little hooks into which it is possible to stitch, in order to secure the ends firmly.

(80C). A plaited braid, attached with small slanting stitches taken into alternating edges of the braid. Russia braids can be sewn down with tiny stitches down the centre.

(80D). Short lengths of rough, smooth or check purl, forming satin stitches taken across a padding composed of rows of string.

(80E). To cover a padded shape with satin stitch using rough, smooth or check purl, which is cut into short pieces, graduated in length to fit the shape.

(80F). To sew tubular braids, use a very fine needle and thread. The stitches pass across, through the braid. At the ends about 2 cm is left, and a tiny slit made in the fabric, through which the end is taken with the aid of a sling, it can be stuck back on the reverse side.

(80G). Raised chain band can be worked with purl, cut to the required lengths, upon a foundation of raised horizontal stitches. By extending these stitches, and increasing the number of rows of chainband an attractive filling is created.

(80H). Passing and other fine threads can be couched down to form many different patterns, these spirals and wavy lines are examples. Surface buttonhole stitch produces a lace-like texture.

81. Metal threads couched with silk, the design sprayed on to the fabric. June Lovesey.

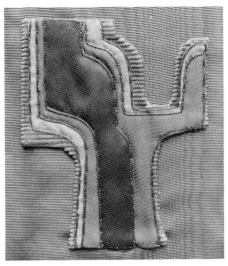

82A–B. Tree of Life – (above) worked out experimentally, with string and studs, sprayed gold – also (left) carried out in applied needle cord, dull satin, silk overcard, with couched gold thread. Jill Friend.

83. 1. English Quilting.

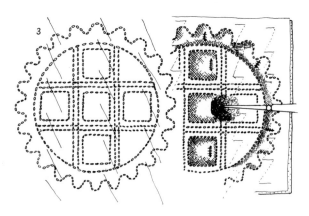

84. 2. Italian Quilting.

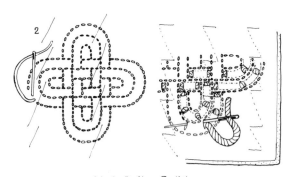

85. 3. Trapunto.

118

Quilting

Quilting sometimes forms the main decoration upon vestments, but more often it is combined with other embroidery. Mainly a popular secular technique, it is for this reason important when designing for the church that the sacred purpose must be uppermost in the designer's mind. It takes thought, imagination and discrimination to produce a satisfactory result. Because quilting has such strong domestic associations special care is needed to avoid the suggestion of a parallel between, for instance, a cope and a dressing gown.

There are three different methods, these can be adapted in various ways, and they can be worked in the hand or in the frame. Whether there are two or three layers of material, they are tacked together with vertical rows of zig-zag tacking. Stab stitching is used for the outlining, the needle is kept straight and enters the material in a single movement, whether running or back stitches. Machine stitching is perfectly satisfactory.

Quilter's marker pens solve the problem of tracing-on the design, as this can be done on the right side of the fabric. Otherwise it is drawn on with tailor's chalk, or the line is tacked or scratched with the needle. The line which results from painting it too thick to be covered by the stitching, consequently the pricking, pouncing and painting method is used on the reverse side of a muslin backing. To produce backstitching on the front, stem stitch is worked on the reverse side.

(83). English Quilting. Tack together the three layers – the top silk – wadding or polyester or acrylic stiffening which is lighter, otherwise domette – and the muslin backing. Stitch together around the outline.

For Italian Quilting, the two layers of fabric, silk and muslin backing, are tacked together and the two parallel design outlines are stitched. Then with a large needle, thick soft wool or cotton is threaded through from the back as shown in the (84).

(85). Trapunto Quilting is padded in small areas, the top silk and backing of unbleached calico are tacked together, and the outline worked, tiny slits are cut in the backing through which the padding enters, the diagram shows the wadding being pushed in with the help of a stiletto, the slit is then stitched together.

Appliqué

Perhaps the most useful of the embroidery methods is appliqué, especially for church vestments and soft furnishing, because of its suitability for large scale undertakings, speed of execution and comparative simplicity, although it can be carried to extremes of elaboration when other techniques are incorporated.

86. *Easter Altar Frontal, detail. Designed and worked by Marjorie Coffey.*
Machine stitched couched synthetic threads which outline the padded shapes.
Magenta and red on yellow. St George's Episcopal Church, Washington, D.C.

One aspect of the work is that it is often planned spon-
taneously and created 'in situ', by cutting out and pinning in
place on the background the shapes, in their colours and textures, thereby making it possible to judge the total effect.

These pieces may even be directly stuck in place with liquid
fabric adhesive, if the use is temporary, the addition of machine
or hand stitching adds durability.

Appliqué can be carried out flatly on a table, but it is better to
frame-up the background material or the backing (if there is one).
The prevention of puckering is important, so it is vital that the

120

grain of the piece of material to be applied and the grain of the background correspond exactly (88). (The exception being for patterned fabrics.)

The design can be built up free-hand with paper or fabric cut into shapes which are pinned to the background or the design is drawn out on paper, in either case the outline is traced (see transferring) or tacked on to the background.

To prevent fraying, iron-on interfacing is pressed on to the back of the pieces of material to be applied, and the design (reversed) is traced on the back, or on the right side – or a template may have been pinned on, and tacked round, after this the shapes are cut out, for a fraying material pure rubber solution may be applied to the cut edges.

The pieces to be applied are then pinned in position on the background and 1. tacked in place, 2. attached with fabric adhesive or 3. bonded with a fusible interlining.

The edges may be overcast with small stitches, herringbone-stitched or machine-stitched with the sewing needle or zig-zag stitched. Other hand embroidery stitches can be used.

BLIND APPLIQUÉ

This method is accurate and is preferable for church work as it is more durable for vestments and soft furnishings which have hard wear. It is not suitable for thick materials. The preparation is as follows:

1. Frame-up the background fabric.
2. Trace on, tack or draw with tailor's chalk, the outline of the design on to the background.
3. Trace the shapes upon the non-stick side of iron-on interfacing, reversing the tracing. Use non-stick interfacing (Vilene), for thin materials. Cut out.

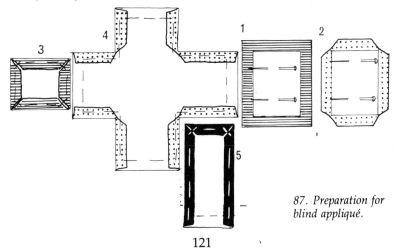

87. *Preparation for blind appliqué.*

88. Preparation for appliqué.

4. Place these templates on the material with the grain running in the same direction as the grain of the background, pin. Or, if interfacing is not being used, trace the outline.
5. Cut out, leaving turnings, as in (87.1, 2).
6. Fold the turning over on to the interlining and tack all round those shapes which are on top (87.3). Do not turn in those turning which will be under other shapes (87.4, 5).
7. Starting with those pieces of the design which are underneath, pin them on to the background fabric (88) and run stitch on the outline.
8. Follow these shapes by those which are on top (89).
9. All the edges which have folded turnings are invisibly slip stitched (39b). This can be seen in the illustration of the pulpit fall.

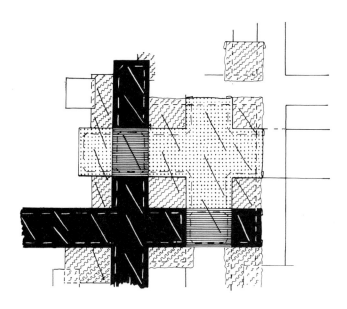

89. Processes in the preparation of the Pulpit Fall carried out in appliqué for St Mary, East Guldeford, Sussex. Beryl Dean.

Patchwork

In recent years patchwork has undergone a revival, stimulated, in part, by the ever widening choice in textured and printed fabrics, also the introduction of man-made fibres and the increased importation of Thai and other Oriental silks. And the range of exciting colours has contributed.

This exclusively secular technique has been extended to include works for cathedrals and churches. Avril Colby was the pioneer, with her beautifully conceived and planned cope and mitre for Burford Church in Devon, and there have been other well designed, interesting examples of patchwork produced for the church. But there have been lamentable failures – instances where the worker has mastered the technique, but has neither the ability nor the understanding to see beyond the limits of tradition towards a well considered design, suitable for its sacred purpose. This has, alas, led to copes and frontals too closely related to bedspreads.

When contemplating the designing of patchwork, it has to be considered as a joining together of individual shapes to form a unified whole. To begin, the overall shape of the object should be determined, then, how the area will be cut up by the main construction lines of the design. These larger shapes are then composed of units formed from the joining together of individual pieces.

The important design lines are further accented and defined by the conscious arrangement of the tonal colour values. For the construction of the design the strongest contrast is planned, and larger areas of lesser importance the tones of similar value can be grouped together.

This may become clearer if an actual example is cited, i.e., the altar frontal illustrated (90). For this design some quality in the

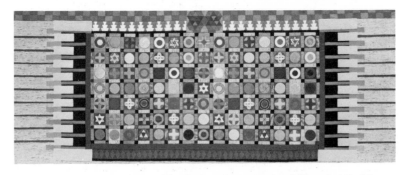

90. *Altar frontal commissioned for the interdenominational Chapel of the Westminster Hospital – 1969. Beryl Dean assisted by Elizabeth Elvin. Patchwork in many different fabrics, including metallic gauze. (Photo: Millar & Harris.)*

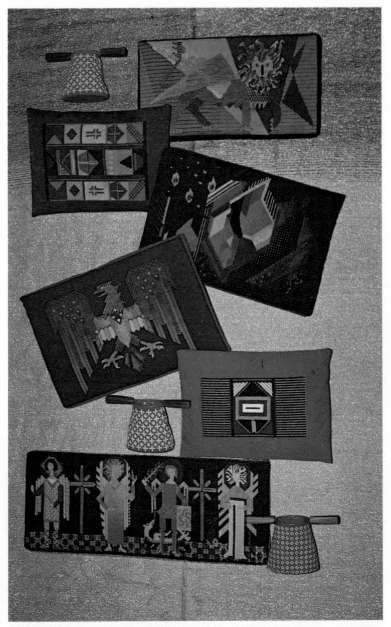

Choir stall cushions, designed by Sylvia Green, St Michaels, Highgate, London.

Left-hand panel entitled 'Vegetation' of a triple screen designed by Hannah Frew Paterson (Also see pages four and five). Photo©Glasgow Museums and Art Galleries.

Multi-seasonal altar frontal for Summerfields School, Oxford, by Judy Barry and Beryl Patten. Design based on the idea of growing corn and the tree of knowledge, 1979.

large Venetian painting which dominated the altar led to the idea that patchwork should be the idiom chosen for the interpretation which the muted richness of the colours inspired.

An altar is a horizontal rectangle, and this one was rather too wide for the size of the chapel, so, to counteract this tendency, wide panels were planned for both ends, these served to emphasise the centre rectangle, where the small scale embroidered patches are justified by the fact that the worshippers are never too far away to see the detail. The combination of differently shaped patches and the grouping of the colours (which were taken from the painting) is intended to concentrate the interest in the centre as the side panels are composed of neutral fawns, brown and dull gold.

There are several books of reference which give full instructions for patchwork, here only the basic information is given.

The fabrics used for patchwork are chosen for some unique quality, related to this are a few points to bear in mind.

1. Differences in the thickness of materials selected for the patches can be compensated by using thinner or thicker Vilene (or other non-iron on interlining) for the templates, if these are not to be removed on completion of the work.

2. As a general rule, the grain should run in the same direction for as many patches as possible, but there are exceptions, as when patterned materials are used and also when the patches are arranged to exploit the play of light by placing the grain in different directions.

3. Vestments should hang well, in deep folds, therefore to attain this the patchwork has to be composed of fabrics of about the same weight, and should not be too stiff. They are pressed on the back before the tacks and templates are carefully removed, so that the work is disturbed as little as possible. The work is then lined.

It is advisable to master traditional methods before embarking upon the more inventive unconventional variants suggested for banners, etc.

The patches used for traditional work are geometric. The templates (91) are cut very accurately from strong, thick paper. These are placed on the wrong side of the material so that the grain of the fabric runs in the same way in as many patches as possible, and the material is cut out, allowing a narrow turning (about $\frac{1}{2}$ cm). Then, with the template pinned in position the turnings are folded over and tacked, avoiding both knots and backstitches, as shown in the diagram (91.1, 2). To join the prepared patches, put the right sides together and overcast the edges (91.2), using a fine needle and thread. Lightly press the work when complete and remove the templates.

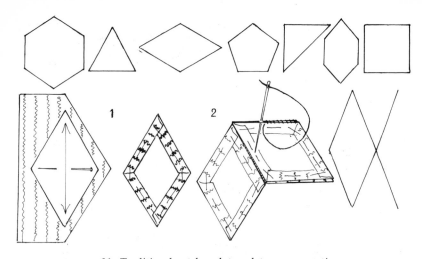

91. Traditional patchwork templates – preparation.

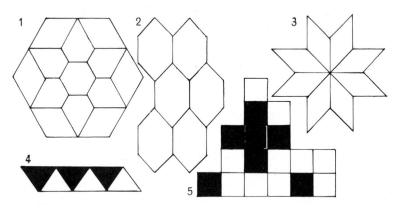

92. Endless are the patterns which can be made with the basic patchwork shapes. – 1. A combination of the diamond, pentagonal shape and hexagon to form the box and star pattern. 2. Church window. 3. Long diamond to make a star. 4. Dog's tooth pattern. 5. Many all-over patterns can be contrived by colour grouping the squares.

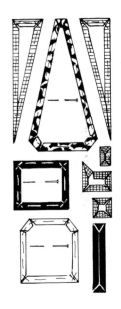

93. *Patchwork composed of irregular shapes.*

This method has to be adapted when realising modern designs in terms of patchwork. As the shapes (patches) will be irregular and the design unlikely to be symmetrical, the tracing of the outline of the design must be reversed when used for cutting each individual template.

Both the direction of the top and the bottom must be marked on each piece.

Then each template is placed upon its piece of fabric, with the selvedge grain running downwards, wherever possible (93A) (except where a detail from a printed pattern is to be used). They are cut out allowing turnings, and tacked (93A).

As this method is likely to be decided upon for altar frontals, pulpit falls, etc., it may be an advantage not to remove the templates, in which case various thicknesses of non-iron Vilene are used. When a particular patch is much thicker than others, it may be necessary to pare that template down a little.

It is much more difficult to overcast together these irregular shapes, than it is to sew the straight sides of the traditional templates. But the result and textural quality gained by carrying out a design in this way, makes the effort worth while. Surface stitchery can be added.

Finally, having lightly pressed the work on the back, and with the tacks removed, the turnings are lightly stuck down to the Vilene (hot iron-on for preference).

127

Mola work

Through tourism this unique type of work has become more widely known. The molas are rectangular embroidered panels which form the front and back of blouses, they are decorated in this unique method – almost appliqué in reverse. Several layers of brightly coloured cotton materials are used, which are cut away to reveal the colour underneath.

These attractive and highly individual designs could well inspire adaptations which might be carried out in the form of church hangings, banners or pulpit falls. The brlliance of the colour would introduce an exciting focal point.

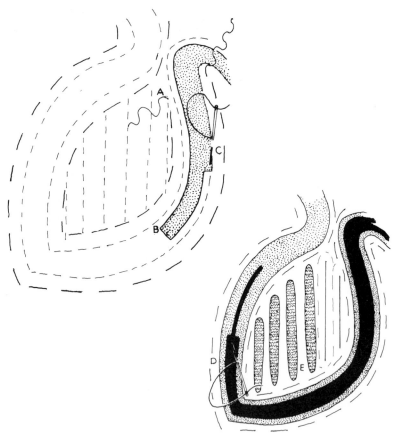

94. To work a detail from a Mola.

128

95. Detail from Mola.

Usually about five or more layers of material are placed one over the other and held together with tacks. The outline of the design is lightly marked on the top layer.

(94) is a detail taken from the illustration (95) and shows at (A) the top layer which is red, on it the outline has been traced. At a little distance from the outline there is a line of tacking. Also shown is a portion cut away, leaving a turning (B). And at (C) is shown the turning folded under and hemmed with tiny stitches, through all the layers.

The next colour, orange, is now exposed, and this is cut leaving a turning which is also folded under and stitched (D). This has revealed the black foundation rectangle of fabric. (Only three whole layers were used.)

In some modern examples, between the first and second layers, small areas of additional coloured material are tacked, they are placed where needed. Here (E) a bright pink has been inserted under the centre of the leaf shape, long slits were cut in the first layer, then hemmed.

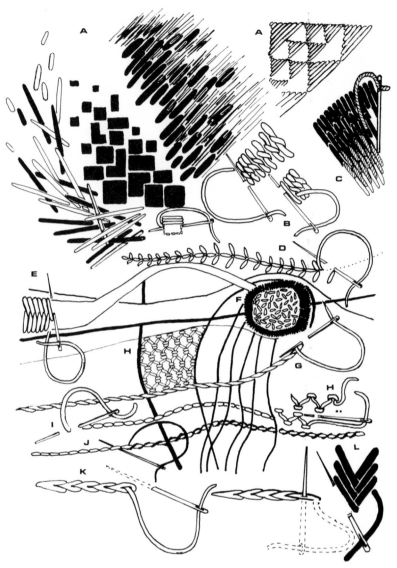

96. *A selection of mainly hand-worked stitches.*

8

Decorative Stitchery

When used imaginatively the characteristics of hand stitches are invaluable for the interpretation of creative design for Ecclesiastical embroidery.

Decorative hand stitches combine well with gold work, adding textural contrast and introducing colour; many are interesting in themselves, yet quite different effects can be achieved when several rows are worked either close together or with a narrow space between. This repetition, especially upon a curve, produces a rhythm, as the light catches the gleam of the thread.

Narrow braids, ribbons or thongs can be used in conjunction with hand (or machine) line stitches, many imaginative examples can be observed in church embroidery from West Germany.

In the following diagrams the working of a selection of stitches is given. When the process has been mastered, try working the same stitch with threads of many different thicknesses and textures, vary both the size, spacing and width. This should lead to further experimentation, explore the possibilities of carrying out a design entirely in one stitch, but changing the threads. With experience it will be found that some metal threads can be used for working the stitches. Another form of contrast is produced by juxtaposing precision and repetition with irregularity in execution and threads.

Most stitches are more easily worked in the hand, but for others an embroidery frame is essential.

To have the correct type and size of needle in relation to the thread and fabric is important, these are: Crewel needles, sizes 5–10, they have a sharp point and longish eye, and are used for most types of embroidery. For canvas work, wool or stranded cotton, and thicker threads tapestry needles are used, they have blunt points, 20 is a useful size. Chenille needles are similar, but have a sharp point. Beading needles are very long and thin with a tiny eye. A double thread is always used. Leather needles have a triangular, sharp bevelled point. Carpet and packing needles being thick and heavy are suitable for string and cords, and are used for framing up.

Flat, mainly line stitches (96).

(A) Satin stitch is the same on top as underneath, to get a precise, slightly raised shape, first outline with running or back stitches. To work a line the stitches are close together and can be vertical or slanting. Worked as groups of counted threads, all over patterns are formed (A). Stitches can be angled to express curves. Or, as in the diagram (A) straight stitches, using threads of different thicknesses would all be worked in one direction. The possibilities are endless.

(B) Roumanian stitch can be varied in width and spacing.

(C) See illustration (19, left). Gradation of colour can be produced by working long and short stitch. Use an embroidery frame, and make one long and one short stitch alternately for the outside or first row, then for the second row bring the needle up, through the previous stitch, half way along its length, and make a long stitch, repeat, taking care that the up and down is kept.

(D) Fern stitch, can be varied in several ways.

(E) Flat stitch produces a wide, solid line.

(F) For this seeding single running stitches are made at random, for white work one tiny back stitch followed by another, over the first, is more effective. The satin stitches of the outline radiate from the centre, and are worked over a split outline, stitched.

(G) Stem stitch, the needle should come up through the hole made by the previous stitch. Many rows, worked close together, or leaving a space between will form an attractive filling.

(H) Chevron stitch, worked either as a line or as a filling is useful.

(I) For the working of Backstitch, the needle enters the fabric at the point at which the previous stitch has ended. This forms the basis for several variations, for example when whipped as at (J).

(K) This diagram shows Split Stitch as worked in the hand, but is more quickly and satisfactorily carried out with a frame. An untwisted thread gives the best results. The needle must come up through the previous stitch at the centre.

(L) Fishbone can be worked close together or wide apart.

(97M) Double Smyrna Cross, an evenly woven fabric makes these filling stitches easier to work, this is done by making a cross stitch over 4 or 8 threads, then work an oblong cross vertically, followed by a cross vertically, followed by a horizontal oblong cross. Over this make a straight cross.

(N) Oblong Smyrna Cross. First work an oblong diagonal cross stitch and make an oblong straight cross over it.

(O) Irregular Herringbone stitches worked with threads of different thicknesses.

(98A) To work Sword-edging stitch, bring the needle out as shown in diagram   (98) and take it down at the point marked X, then bring it up on the right-hand side.

132

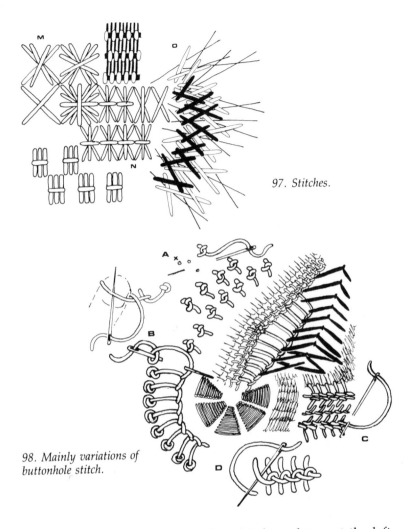

97. Stitches.

98. Mainly variations of buttonhole stitch.

(B) Knotted buttonhole. The thread is brought up at the left hand and is then passed once round the thumb of the left hand, whilst holding the material, transfer the loop so formed, on to the needle, by passing it up through the loop, see the sketch on the left of the diagram. Continue to work the buttonhole stitch in the usual way.

(C) Slanting buttonhole. As an alternative this can be crossed by slanting the needle in the reverse direction for the next stitch.

Buttonhole stitch can be worked over thick wool, other threads, narrow ribbon, braid or thongs laid on the surface.

(D) Loop stitch.

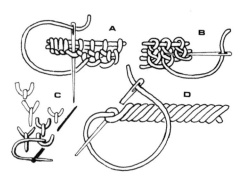

99. Stitches.

(99A) The first row of Detached buttonhole stitches are either worked over a foundation of two long satin stitches or a row of small back-stitches. The buttonhole stitches only enter the fabric at the beginning and end of each row.

(B) For Ceylon stitch the working is similar to that for (A), except that the thread is looped into the previous row.

(C) Fly stitch.

(D) To work Rope stitch, follow the diagram, but hold down the thread near to its start, towards the left with the thumb and throw the remainder of the thread over to the right, before inserting the needle just below the starting point and a little to the left.

Diagram (100) shows some of the alternatives possible when working buttonhole stitch. These add interest when combined with gold work or appliqué.

(A) Cretan stitch, after completing the working as shown in the diagram, put the needle in position towards the centre, with the thread on the left. Changes of spacing and width are possible.

(B) Wave stitch.

(C) Ladder stitch, can be used to make a wide line or repeated, side by side with additional horizontal satin stitches to make an attractive filling, capable of infinite variety.

(101A) Single feather stitch.

(B) Double feather.

(C) The working of Chained Feather stitch can be followed from the diagram, it will be seen that the needle points towards the centre each time.

(D) For Closed Feather the stitches must alternate, the needle is inserted exactly below the previous stitch. It is effective to work over a bunch of laid threads of a contrasting colour.

134

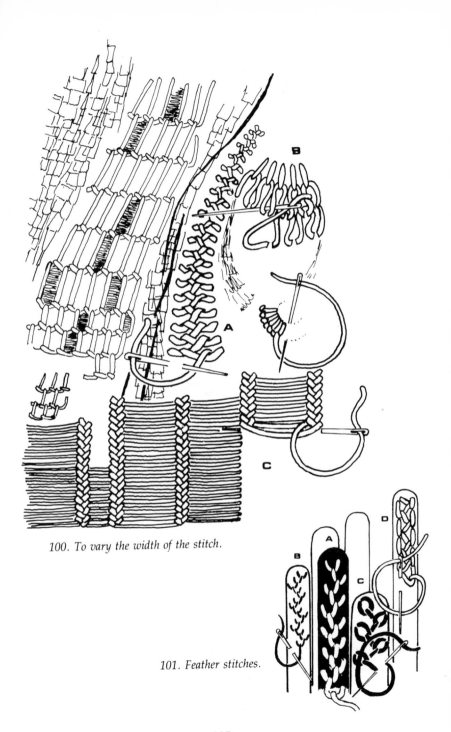

100. *To vary the width of the stitch.*

101. *Feather stitches.*

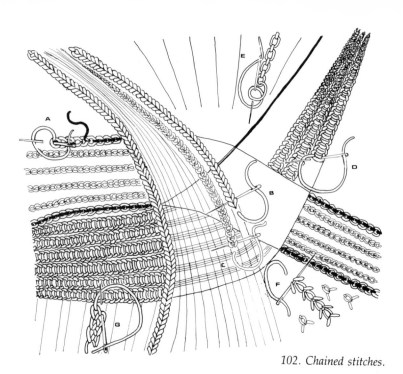

102. Chained stitches.

Diagram (102A) shows the working of Chain stitch, together with Back stitch in a contrasting colour. To produce Zig-zag Chain each loop is worked at an angle to the previous one.

(B) Heavy chain. Bring the thread through at the commencement of the line. Take a short running stitch and bring the needle through again as if for a second, but instead of taking another, pass the needle under the first stitch and take it to the back again at the first point where it came through. So the first loop of the chain is formed. Bring the needle to the front again upon the line a step farther along, and then pass it as before, under the stitch behind, which this time is the chain loop. Next pass the needle a second time under the first stitch as before.

(C) The start of the working of Broad chain is similar to that of Heavy chain, but it will be seen that the needle is taken back once, not twice as in Heavy chain. It is necessary to progress with small stitches.

(D) Both the width and spacing of Open chain can be varied.

(E) Cable stitch. Having brought the thread through, with the thumb of the left hand, hold it down upon the material below the starting point and a little to the right. Next pass he needle under the held thread in the direction from left to right, and pass the

136

thread through until only a small loop is left lying on the material. Insert the needle in the centre of the loop, release the held-down thread and bring the needle through to the surface a little below where it entered and outside the loop. Take hold of the working thread with the right hand and pull it, in order to tighten the loop that is now upon the needle, and pass the thread round, under the point of the needle, and lay it upon the material up to the left side, as shown in the diagram. Then with the left thumb upon the stitch in the process of making and pull the thread through. The first loop can be made by a twist of the needle round the thread, and it is the quicker way of two.

(F) Wheat-Ear. This can be followed from the diagram (F).

(G) Double chain. To start, work an Open chain loop and into this another one, putting it to the left of the first. Next insert the needle a second time into the centre of the first Chain loop and bring it out below, but on the right side. Pull the needle through over the working thread. For the fourth stitch, throw the thread across the left and insert the needle in the centre of the second Chain loop, to the left of the thread; this stage is illustrated in the diagram.

Knotted stitches (103)

For their textural quality the knotted stitches are invaluable, and they can be varied by using threads of different thicknesses.

(A) Four-legged Knot stitch. The working method can be followed from the diagram.

(B) When starting to work a French Knot, bring the thread through and hold it taut with the thumb and finger of the left hand. Let the point of the needle encircle the held thread twice,

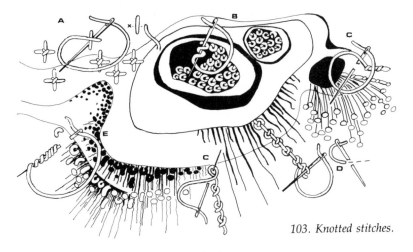

103. Knotted stitches.

as shown in the drawing, then, with the twists upon the point kept fairly tight by holding firmly on to the thread, revolve the needle round until the point is close to where the thread first came through. Pass the needle and thread through the twists to the back of the material.

(C) and (C) Two variations of Coral stitch. The appearance can be changed by the angle of the needle and the way in which the thread is pulled up.

(D) Double Knot. To start, make a small slanting stitch passing under the traced line, then the thread is slipped under the short first stitch. For the second time the needle takes the thread under the same stitch, as for a Buttonhole stitch, it then continues as shown in the diagram.

(E) Bullion knot. Having brought the thread to the surface of the fabric insert the needle on the line and bring it through again where it first came out. Push the needle through so that it can be wound round the thicker end, then place the thumb lightly upon it and pull the thread through. When it is tight, pass the needle and thread over, so that they point in the opposite direction. Tighten up the thread and pass it to the back, down through the point at which it first came through.

(104). The fringed edges of woven fabrics can be knotted in many ways. There is scope for inventive experimentation.

(A) shows an original treatment of a fringe (a detail of a hanging from the U.S.A.) which could incorporate Turk's head knots. To make the knot use a firm, rather wiry thread. To begin, arrange the thread in a kind of double loop, as seen in the (diagram 104.B).

(B) Hold this arrangement of loops at the base between the left-hand finger and thumb, and then pass the needle in and out of them, as shown. Before finally pulling the needle through, tighten up the loops a little whilst they are around it, as, at first, they are usually too large for the completed ball. This knot, as shown in the diagram, with the needle through it, represents the framework of the ball and should be about the required size. After the original loops have been tightened up, the needle pulls the thread through them and then proceeds to continue threading in and out of the partly formed ball, by following the lead started by the dotted line in the diagram. This entails exactly following the lead of the original thread from start to finish, passing over and under the various loops in the same way. This continues until three rows of thread lie side by side, whilst doing this it must be coaxed into a rounded form. Care must be taken to keep the needle on the inside of the thread it is following.

(C) A decorative fringe made with narrow ribbons, cords and

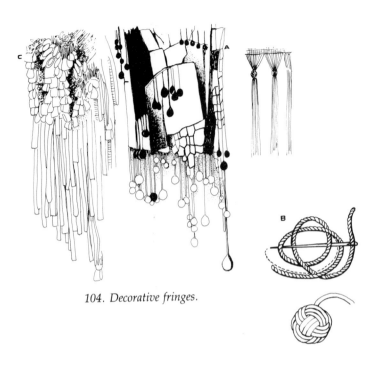

104. Decorative fringes.

threads. The time has come for reappraisement of the creation of fringes, (104A and C are given as possible examples).
Interesting fringes can, if designed for the purpose, form a good finish to banners, falls, hangings and stoles.

Composite stitches (105) are worked in one or more stages.

(A) Raised stem stitch band combines well with gold work. First laid stitches are worked vertically, more are put in the centre to raise it, over this horizontal stitches are worked at intervals. Finally rows of stem stitches are worked over the foundation.

(B) Two parallel rows or alternating back stitches form the foundation of Interlaced band stitch, after making a stitch as shown in the diagram, the needle points upwards when going into the bottom row.

(C) Twisted lattice can be used as a filling or as a line stitch. The diagonal foundation stitches are laid in one direction, then those in the other direction are darned under and over. Next the needle passes up under one transverse thread, and then down under the next, for this the needle points downwards.

(D) Pekinese stitch can be varied, both in the size of the back stitches and the loops which pass through them, as shown in the (105D).

139

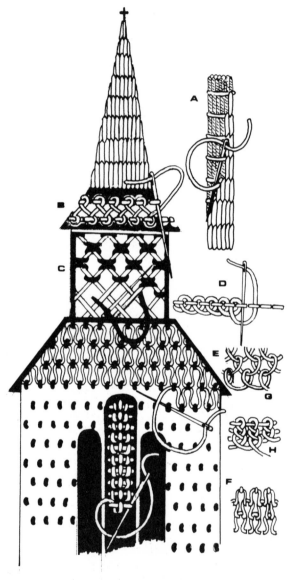

105. *Open filling stitches.*

(E) For Cloud filling a basis of isolated stitches is spaced regularly over the surface. Then the thread is passed in a zig-zag, horizontally across shape. There are several variations of this stitch.

(F) To start wave filling, make tiny upright stitches into the fabric, from right to left, take the needle through the material at the base and through the stitches of the previous row to form the filling.

(G) To work buttonhole filling, make a row of stitches into the fabric, then do buttonhole stitches into the loops of the previous row. The needle only enters the background at the beginning and end of each row.

(H) For Ceylon filling form one or more foundation stitches, then slip the needle from right to left, behind each loop in the previous row. It is detached from the ground except at the beginning and end of each line.

LAID WORK

There are certain characteristics which give to laid work its own identity. The smooth, flat surface catches the light according to

106. Laid work.

141

the direction of the threads. And the texture depends upon the type of thread, for example stout floss laid horizontally contrasted with stranded cotton worked diagonally would be interesting. The way in which the colours can be changed or arranged to produce gradation is another valuable characteristic. Richness is produced by stitching the tying down with couched metal threads (106.7) in a variety of surface patterns to produce solid fillings. Many decorative open fillings can be invented, these could be worked in metal threads with the addition of rough or check purl (6).

This is one of the techniques for which an embroidery frame is essential. The diagram (106.1) shows that a long stitch crosses the surface from side to side, the needle comes up immediately beside the point at which the previous stitch has entered the fabric, and the needle is taken down as near as possible to the last stitch, on the outline, so that there is only a tiny stitch on the reverse side. When worked as a solid filling the edge can be either hard or broken to give a soft effect (4). To change the colour the stitches are spaced (2), the long laid foundation stitches are tied down with a long stitch taken at right angles, using a finer thread, which, in its turn is couched down at regular intervals with a tiny stitch (3), (4).

Most open laid fillings are based upon a foundation of long stitches which are crossed and tied down at the intersections with a small stitch.

Whole areas can be covered with long laid stitches either in self colour or in several colours, the change of direction gives an interesting play of light upon the thread (8).

107. Needle weaving.

142

108. Torah Mantle designed and embroidered by Joan Koslan Swartz (1972) for Chapel Cong Emanuel, San Francisco, California.

NEEDLE WEAVING

Needle weaving has been developed imaginatively for the decoration of vestments in Britain and in the U.S.A. Basically it is the traditional method (107) which is used, but for the large shaped areas of the pattern it may be necessary to insert additional foundation threads. The weaving can be carried out in threads of different textures, see illustration (108), this example shows a most imaginative development of needle weaving on a large scale.

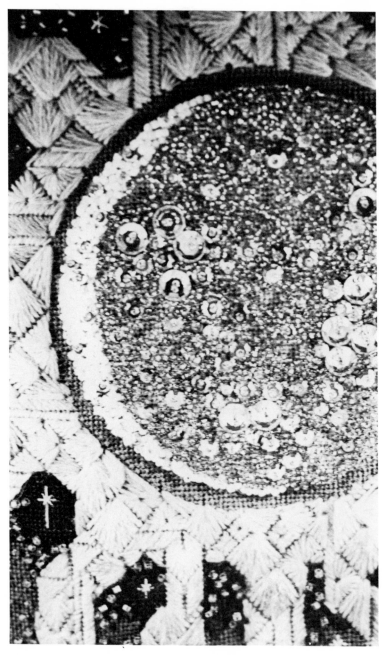

109. Mitre, worked in a variety of canvas stitches, wool, stranded cotton and metal threads. Executed by Priscilla Leonard.

109A. Designer, Sylvia Green.

9

Canvas work for kneelers, cushions, etc.

Kneelers, hassocks, cushions, and alms bags, etc., are generally carried out in canvas work, so called because the stitches are worked upon a foundation of canvas. (The term Tapestry is wrongly applied, as it is woven on a loom, and needle point is also incorrect, because this is fine, needle-made lace.) Canvas work is a popular type of embroidery, as it is simple to do, yet affords tremendous scope for the creative experienced embroiderer.

Many people enjoy the discipline imposed by the canvas foundation, and the resultant somewhat rigid design, which can, nevertheless, be very attractive.

The type of design referred to is particularly satisfactory for projects to be carried out by a group of many individual workers, as a combination of simple geometric patterns can be most attractive, affording latitude in the stitch selection.

More interestingly there is the spontaneous approach to canvas work, which gives scope for an imaginative interpretation of the design, and requires judgement in the choice of stitches which will capture the essence of the design, thereby testing the creative skill of the embroiderer.

It is the durability of canvas work which makes the technique specially suitable for kneelers, and is its main characteristic. Although this does not apply when the method is used for decorative pictures or hangings, for this purpose the inclusion of long surface stitches is justified.

When designing kneelers it is vital that the scheme, as a whole, should belong in character to the interior of the church and its furnishings. The introduction of pattern and colour around or before the altar and on the floor, can add welcome interest. Because the kneelers or hassocks contribute greatly to the overall appearance of the cathedral or church the design must be good. Therefore the emphasis should be upon the design and its composition, whether abstract, geometric or based upon a more representational theme. Originality in the approach to the designs and to the interpretation is valuable. Too many schemes have failed in this respect because of the poor, feeble and unimaginative designs, resulting in a waste of time, effort and money.

Because it is the visual impact of the total effect of a colourful scheme which is of the utmost importance, it is therefore a job for the trained designer, one who can visualise the finished result. Any such project needs a trained leader to control and keep the unity necessary for artistic success, yet this leader should encourage each individual contributor to the scheme and allow as much scope for initiative as possible.

MATERIALS

There are two types of canvas, single or double thread (penelope). The single weave is usually preferable as it will take a greater variety of stitches and is easier to count.

Canvas is identified according to the number of threads to 5 cm (or to 1 inch). A fine canvas has 34 threads to 5 cm. It is sold by the metre, and there are several widths.

The more expensive linen canvas is recommended for kneelers, etc.

Threads used for working kneelers must withstand hard wear, crewel, tapestry or the fine French or Florentine (when obtainable) wools and Wilton carpet thrums are suitable. The number of threads used is important as the canvas must be well covered, but without being lumpy, which is the result of using threads too thick for the size of canvas.

Tapestry needles are used for this embroidery, they have a long eye and blunt point. A fairly short length of wool should be threaded into the needle, as a long one wears thin.

Preparing the work

Allowing for a wide surrounding margin of canvas, cut the rectangle to the required size. If it is to be worked in the hand, the edges are bound. But the result is more satisfactory when a frame is used, for this bind the two side edges, then frame-up.

When the design is geometric in character, it is drawn out on graph paper and worked by counting either the threads or the holes of the canvas.

Alternatively the transferring is carried out by first outlining the drawn design with a strong black line, then put this underneath, in contact with the underside of the canvas (books form a firm surface on which to draw). The design can be seen through the canvas, and it is outlined better with pen or brush, waterproof ink is preferable.

Method:

To begin make a knot in the thread which is taken through a short distance from the starting point, then bring it up ready for the first stitch (110A), as the work proceeds the end is secured. To join, the old thread is brought up, and the new thread (shown threaded into the needle in the diagram) is started as before, the ends being worked in. The knots are cut off.

There are a great many different canvas stitches, the choice of just the right one for the purpose depends upon the scale of the stitch in relation to the area to be covered, and to the size of the canvas. The textural quality of the stitch also has to be considered, whether flat or a raised surface is needed, and these can be varied according to the threads used. In the diagrams an attempt has been made to illustrate some of these points. (110 and 111 give stitches with contrasting textures). Tent stitch has a flat surface and is more even when worked diagonally (B), an alternative method of stitching over a laid thread is shown at (C) and a knobbly texture, (D) a double straight cross is worked over four threads of the canvas. Eye stitches are also introduced. The contrast between flat and raised surfaces is most effective, even when the work is carried out in monotone, if velvet stitch is included, it can be worked with a single thick thread or a bunch of threads, from the (111E) it will be seen that the thread is taken round a knitting needle or strip of plastic. When complete the loops of each row are cut to form a pile. A single row of longer loops make a fringe.

The stitches put together in diagram (112) all have somewhat definitive directional textures. Encroaching Gobelin (F) is composed of oblique stitches which in this example go over 4 horizontal and 2 vertical threads of the canvas. In direct contrast is the pile created by several rows of Turkey knots, for clarity, a single thread is shown at (G) in the drawing, but a bunch of threads would actually be used, the loops are cut at the end. Straight cross (H) is worked over two threads in each direction. Upright Gobelin (I), and the diagonal satin stitches with backstitching, can be worked from the diagram (J). A smooth surface results from working Florentine stitch, (K) in the diagram the small cross marks the point at which the needle will come up. The laid foundation thread helps to cover the canvas and accentuates the horizontal ridges characteristic of this (L) variation of upright Gobelin.

At present there is a trend towards the soft merging of one ground stitch into another, such an example is shown in (113). This type of scheme is carried out using very thick weaving or knitting wools contrasted with finer cotton or silk threads (not shown here). The Eye stitches could be outlined with backstitches. The Algerian eye (M) is made by working twice into the centre, from the corners and the middle of the sides of the square. At (N) a small cross shows where the thread will enter the canvas

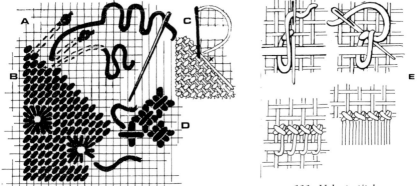

110. Starting and joining the thread for canvas work.

111. Velvet stitch.

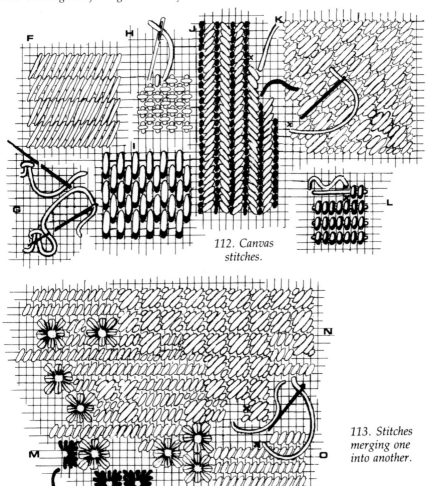

112. Canvas stitches.

113. Stitches merging one into another.

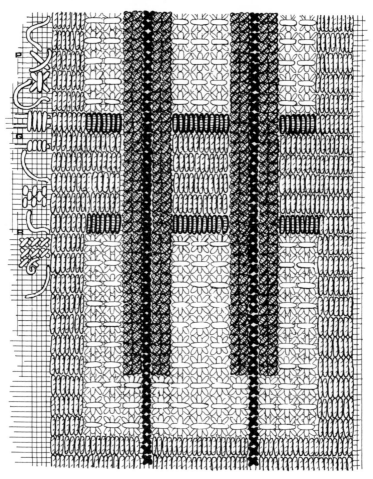

114. For the geometric design.

to complete the stitch, for this variation of Mosaic stitch (O). This form of Gobelin makes attractive ridges when a thick thread is used.

A possible combination of stitches which could be used for a geometric design (114). Smyrna or Double cross (P) can be followed from the drawing, as can the variations of Upright Gobelin (Q). Cross stitches (R) are made from the bottom right to the top left, over two threads in each direction, and cross in the reverse direction. Greater strength results when the stitches are individually completed, instead of working along a row in one direction, and returning to complete each stitch.

In (115) is shown at (S) small straight crosses over two threads alternate with diagonal crosses over four threads of the canvas. Plaited Gobelin; the stitches all face in the same direction for one row and in the opposite way for the next. Rice, or Crossed Corners can be followed from the diagram (U), it covers the ground quickly. (V and W) are variations of the Hungarian stitch, and (X) is Mosaic, which is small in scale.

When the embroidery has been finished, it will only need to be dampened on the back, whilst still in the frame, it is then left to dry for about twenty-four hours. But if the canvas is misshapen the work has to be stretched. This method also applies for many other types of embroidery.

Cover a board or corner of a wooden surface with an old clean cloth, on this place the embroidery face downwards with one straight selvedge edge to the edge of the board, pin or nail at intervals, then pull the opposite side, and put in nails, repeat for the top and bottom, checking to see that it is accurate, and that any lines on the design are straight. Then thoroughly dampen with a sponge and water and leave to dry for twenty-four hours (116).

When the work is not badly puckered or out of shape, it can be pinned out upon a damp cloth or sheets of blotting paper and left to dry.

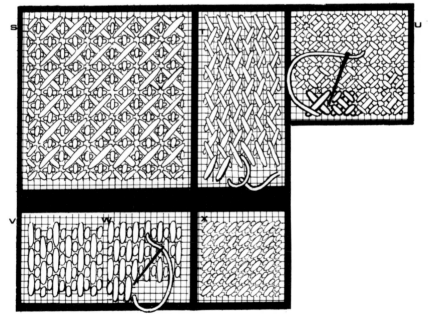

115. Plaited Gobelin, etc.

151

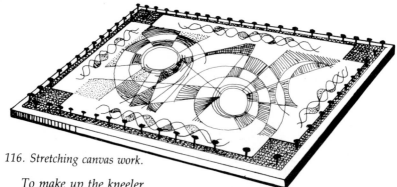

116. *Stretching canvas work.*

To make up the kneeler

When the kneeler has been worked in one piece, cut it out leaving good turnings on the canvas. Stitch up the corner seams, press flatly nd turn out.

There are several possible fillings, foam rubber or Dunlopillo, resilient plastic foam, and other forms of rubber latex, when any one of these is cut to shape it should be slightly larger than the actual measurement, and it is generally more satisfactory to include one or two layers of thick carpet felt, cut to the actual size. The filling should be covered with calico. It is then pushed inside the embroidery. With the face down, turn the canvas edges over, see (117) and lace across in both directions, using a strong thread.

At this stage attach a ring for hanging, if this is to be included. Neaten the underside of the kneeler or hassock with upholsterer's linen or glazed hessian (Burlap).

Making up the long communion-rail kneelers is properly the upholsterer's job, as it is difficult, but if an attempt is to be made, then construct a kneeler to the exact size plus 10–20 mm, using hessian (burlap) or calico, do not seam up one end. Stretch out this shape upon a wooden surface, and nail the turnings of the base to the wood, the stuffing can then be poked down, making sure that the corners are well padded; when really hard, the open end is sewn up. Long stitches can be taken from top to bottom through the filling, using string, and these can be tied off, this keeps the filling in place. The process for covering the long kneeler is the same as before.

117. *Making up the kneeler –.*

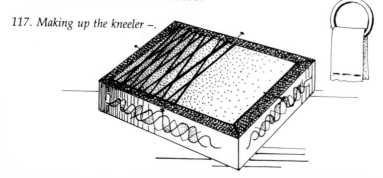

10

Machine Embroidery

In the following pages Hazel Chapman encourages and advises us upon the use of the domestic sewing machine for church embroidery, as so many people have become enthusiastic exponents. Interesting techniques can be speedily and efficiently carried out. Even on the simple straight stitch electric machine, braids and cords can be applied and really intricate linear designs can be carried out with the usual presser foot. However with a zig-zag or 'swing needle' machine the potential is greater, and if extra practical or decorative stitches can be undertaken, then the possibilities are almost limitless.

There is even more potential if the machine is used for 'free embroidery', that is with the sewing foot removed and the feed dog (teeth) out of contact with the fabric. This can be done – depending on the machine, either by lowering or covering the feed dog or by raising the level of the needle plate. On some very old machines that appear to have no means of removing the feed, the teeth can be covered with masking tape to put them out of contact with the fabric. Instructions for this and free embroidery are to be found in the machine hand book and there are many good books available that deal in depth with this aspect of embroidery. Basically it involves stretching the fabric 'drum tight' in a round embroidery frame, removing the sewing foot, and whilst sewing, moving the fabric in any direction desired. It is just like drawing, but the paper (fabric) is moved instead of the pencil (needle).

There are simple, but quick and effective, decorative techniques that can be carried out using the machine as for ordinary sewing, using a sewing foot, therefore making the work very easy to control.

Threads and Yarns for Machine Embroidery

Care should be taken to select threads and yarns that are suitable. Mercerised sewing thread, such as Sylko nos. 40 and 50 or Machine Embroidery Thread nos. 30 and 50 are best for use through the needle (the higher the number the finer the thread).

Sylko is ideal. Not only is it available almost everywhere, it also comes in a wonderful range of over two hundred and fifty colours. Sylko 50 is very similar in weight to no. 30 Machine Embroidery Thread, but much stronger, making it just right for embroidery that needs to be durable as well as beautiful. Machine Embroidery Thread is less widely available, has less strength and offers a limited colour range. It is, however, more lustrous and no. 50 is extremely good for discreet mending, or for fine embroidery on fair linen or on a chalice veil for example. (Man made threads have a tendency to stretch during the process of working, and if the fabric cannot withstand this, it will lead to puckering.)

Heavier yarns with a firm twist (so that they are unlikely to 'fluff') in cotton, linen, wool and metal are ideal for couching purposes. The surfaces of some of the man-made yarns, however beautiful they may look when new, tend to become fluffy and are therefore best avoided on work that will in the long run receive wear. Pearl cotton, such as Sylko Perlé no. 5 for example, is not only useful for hand embroidery, it can be used as a bobbin yarn or for couching with a Multiple Cording Foot. When it is used on the bobbin, the bobbin tension will need to be loosened a little to allow the thicker thread to pass through the tension unit. For machines that use this system, it is wise to purchase an extra bobbin case and keep this especially for embroidery. When working with a heavier thread, such as Sylko Perlé, on the bobbin (other yarns of a similar nature can also be used) it will be the WRONG side of the fabric that is uppermost with the right side away from you on the surface of the machine bed. This means that the design to be embroidered can be clearly marked on the wrong side of the fabric and followed very easily. Refer to the chapter that deals with marking out designs or use the latest fabric marking pen. This is a fibre-tip pen that marks in blue. The marks made can be erased instantly by applying a tiny drop of water with a fine sable or squirrel paint brush. This system is suitable for either washable or dry cleanable fabrics. (Remember to reverse the design so that it appears correct on the right side.)

Metallic yarns look especially effective used in this way as they catch the light and produce unusual textures and shadings – especially when used with shaded thread through the needle. Ask at your embroidery stockist for those suitable for use on the sewing machine bobbin. (There are also some that may be used through the needle.)

Fabrics

Many fabrics are suitable for machine embroidered work. Choose those which are firmly woven, and for a background avoid materials which 'give' or distort easily.

The humidity in some churches varies from time to time and dampness in the air can very often cause fabrics to pucker. One way of helping to cope with this problem is to pre-shrink all

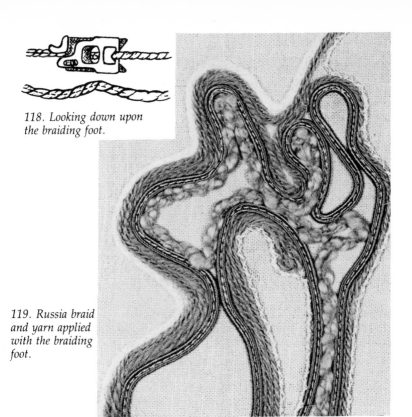

118. *Looking down upon the braiding foot.*

119. *Russia braid and yarn applied with the braiding foot.*

fabrics selected for use before any embroidery takes place. This can be done very easily, for dry cleanable fabric, by rolling it in a slightly damp cloth for twenty-four hours or in the case of washable fabric, by gently washing and drying it according to fabric type. In both cases it will need careful pressing (not ironing) using a pressing cloth before any work is started. Care should be taken not to stretch the fabric in any way. Another way to avoid the chance of puckering is to ensure that, when fabrics are applied to the background, they are placed so that they are exactly 'on grain'. In other words the warp and weft of the applied fabric should lie in exactly the same direction as that of the background fabric. Additionally, it will help if fabrics used together are of the same type. (ie cotton with cotton, wool with wool etc.)

A good choice can be made from the vast ranges of furnishing fabrics available, but plain calico, first well laundered to remove any dressing and then carefully pressed is also excellent and inexpensive. This too has the advantage of readily accepting dyes and certain chosen areas may be coloured with dyes such as Dylon Colour Fun, painted on by hand or permanently transfer dyed using Transcouleur inks.

155

120. Machine stitched with braiding, multiple cording foot and satin stitch.

When selecting yarns and threads for use on these fabrics, do consider textural contrast very carefully. Shiny yarns and applied fabrics look good on a mat background and vice-versa. Lay out the yarns and fabrics on the surface of the background fabric to give an idea of the finished effect. View these from a distance as well as at close range. Something that looks lovely near-to may disappear into insignificance when seen from the back of the church for example. Remember also to consider the colour scheme already in use in the church and make sure that the colours used integrate well with this.

Fine leather pieces, metallic or coloured, suedes, acetate, PVC and velvet can be quickly and easily applied using the blind hem stitch or one similar. In appearance this will look very like work done by hand, but will of course be so very much quicker to carry out.

When doing appliqué work with velvet or other fabrics that are liable to fray, consider using a bonding web (available from stores that offer a good range of sewing aids) to heat bond the fabric in place before stitching. As distinct from blind appliqué, fabric shapes to be applied by machine may also be ironed to a non-woven fusible interlining before being cut out – this will give a clean edge and make them much less liable to fray. Select the interlining according to fabric weight and follow the manufacturer's instructions for use.

156

Needles

For machine embroidery work, choose needles that are compatible with the weight of the fabric, exactly as you would do when handling any sewing job. If anything, it is better to choose a slightly heavier needle – in most instances size 12 or 14 (80 or 90 in Continental sizes) will be ideal. Remember that man made fabrics blunt the needle quickly, so check regularly that it is still sharp. There are special needles available for sewing leather, your sewing machine shop will be able to supply you with these.

Accessories

There are certain accessories that can really make machine embroidery easy. Even though some of them may not be available for your machine, you will often find that those manufactured for other makes will fit your model.

When making enquiries about these, take your usual presser foot along with you so that the sewing machine dealer can advise you about this. (When trying to track down the various accessories, look in the Yellow Pages telephone directory under 'Sewing Machines' and you will find the local shops listed.) By looking at a sewing foot from your machine, a reputable dealer will be able to tell you immediately if any or all of these extra feet can be used on your model.

The Braiding Foot will accommodate a variety of yarns or narrow braids. It has an adjustable channel through which the braid is inserted and a straight or decorative stitch can be used to couch the braid or yarn into position. It can be used on a straight stitch or swing needle machine and is ideal for applying Russia braid and a variety of narrow ribbons and yarns. The braid should be threaded through the foot before it is attached to the machine. (An instruction leaflet is supplied with the foot at the time of purchase.)

The Multiple Cording foot (121) will allow any number up to five fine cords to be run through it for stitching down at one time. These are automatically guided by the foot and can be stitched down using the multiple zig-zag or any other decorative stitch. As with the Braiding Foot, the cords should be threaded through from top to bottom before fixing the foot to the machine. It is a good idea to tie the cords together behind the foot to prevent them pulling out before stitching is started. This foot is also supplied with an instruction leaflet. Suitable for use with fine coloured and metallic yarns.

121. Multiple cording foot.

122. Machine straight stitching with aid of reverse control.

123. Machine stitched textures.

A Transparent All Purpose Foot will enable the stitches to be viewed whilst they are forming – it has areas cut away on the underside to allow for the passage of the embroidery. For use on swing needle machines.

Circular Sewing Devices allow decorative circles to be sewn in a variety of sizes; ideal when symmetry is required. An easy to use and far less expensive circular sewing device however, is to tape a drawing pin – point upmost, to the bed of the machine between the needle and the main body, so that it will act as a pivot for the fabric. The size of the circle depends on the distance that the pin is placed from the needle. A rubber or cork gently pushed on to the point after the fabric has been placed in position will prevent accidental hand injury.

The Darning foot is sold with most machines. It has a small base with a hole in it through which the needle passes. A spring rests against the needle clamp and raises and lowers the foot with every stitch. This enables the fabric to be moved easily under it and stitching can be carried out in any direction. It is used for darning and free embroidery – with or without an embroidery frame (see machine handbook). It can be used with straight stitch and swing needle machines.

The Tacking or Golden Needle is so very useful, both for general tacking and for positioning fabrics to be applied. The zig-zag stitch is used with this and because of the construction of the needle the stitch misses on the left hand swing of the zig-zag and elongates into a very long straight stitch. Ideal for heavy top stitching and tacking. Only for use on swing needle machines.

USING THE 'REVERSE' CONTROL

Most modern electric machines have a reverse control of some kind. On many it is in the form of a button and on others, a lever. By learning to use this whilst the machine is stitching, many lovely designs can be produced. After stitching forwards for a short distance engage the reverse control for the same (or less or more) number of stitches. By repeating this sequence, lines of fine straight or zig-zag stitches can be built up into areas of texture that cover the fabric very quickly.

The fabric should be held firmly in the left hand and gently drawn to the left whilst this backwards and forwards action is taking place. Remember to leave enough fabric outside the area to be embroidered so that you can take a firm grasp on it. Remember also to back the fabric with paper or iron-on interlining as stitching on a single layer of fabric may result in puckering. An example of this embroidery can be seen in (122) which shows lines of shaded straight stitches forming a design based on organ pipes. (123) shows the same technique, but with metallic yarn

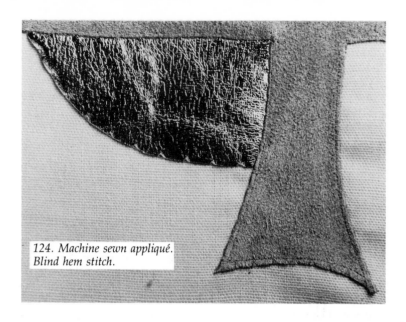

124. *Machine sewn appliqué.*
Blind hem stitch.

used on the bobbin to define the cross design. On a machine with automatic decorative stitches many of these may also be used in this way. The three step zig-zag and blind hem stitch being particularly effective.

USING THE BLIND HEM STITCH FOR APPLIQUÉ (124)

This stitch, really a sequence of stitches, is very quick and useful for applying fray-resistant fabrics and leathers. The sequence generally comprises four straight stitches followed by one zig-zag stitch and by allowing the straight stitches to fall alongside the fabric to be applied and the zig-zag to fall on the applied piece, a very neat finish can be effected. Many modern machines offer other similar stitches – they too can be used in this way. (For applying fabrics that fray very easily it is best to use the zig-zag stitch.) An approximate guide for the stitch setting is width 2 and length 1½–2. (Consult machine handbook for instructions for your particular machine.)

Appliqué method for firm, non-fraying fabrics, suede, P.V.C.,
leather, using the Blind-Hem Stitch
1. Draw shape of fabric to be applied on paper.
2. Place drawn shape on to appliqué fabric and pin, checking to make sure that the grain will lie in the same direction as that of the background fabric.
3. Cut out shape.

4. Pin and tack into place on the background fabric with small stitches.
5. Select a thread such as Sylko 40 or 50 in as close a colour as possible to the fabric to be applied and thread up the machine.
6. Position the work under the foot, so that the straight stitches of the sequence fall alongside the edge of the fabric to be applied. The zig-zag stitch will then stitch over the fabric edge at intervals every four stitches. By reducing the length of stitch, these can be made to fall closer together.

(N.B. Remember that fabrics to be applied can first be heat bonded into position or ironed onto an iron-on interlining to give them body and make them easier to handle.)

Hints for successful work
1. Never sew on a single thickness of fabric. In many instances fabric may be ironed onto a non-woven fusible interlining, ie for pulpit falls, banners and hangings where folds will not appear and the fabric lies flat. Alternatively support the fabric with paper whilst sewing. The perforations made by the needle allow it to be pulled away after stitching has taken place. The rolls of greaseproof paper sold for kitchen use are inexpensive and serve well for this purpose.
2. Plan your designs carefully and be sure that they will work before attempting to machine. Many hours of tedious unpicking can be avoided by the preliminary ground work being right. Make small test samples to try out ideas; any that obviously will not work can then be discarded at an early stage.
3. Don't be too ambitious. Simple designs often prove to be the most effective in the long run.
4. Try to use the best quality materials possible (these need not always be expensive) as it is not worthwhile to spend long hours working with inferior fabrics and threads that will not stand up to a considerable term of service.
5. If necessary embroidery is pressed (not ironed) on its reverse side; it is laid upon a cloth and several thicknesses of padding.

Suppliers:
Transcolour – transfer dye inks from: Ploton Sundries, Archway Road, North London.
Dylon Colour Fun – paint-on fabric dyes from: All main Dylon stockists.
Bondaweb – fabric bonding from stockists of Vilene.

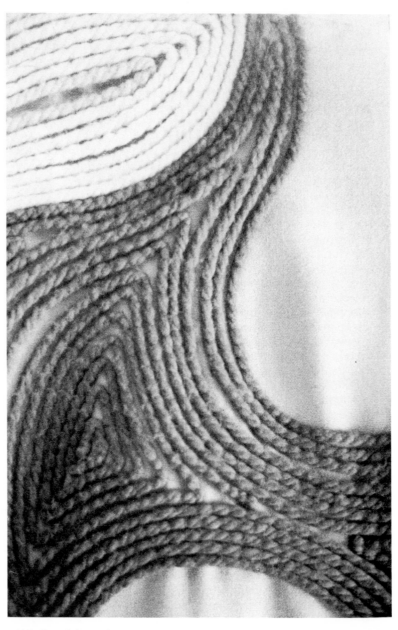

125. *Detail from chasuble by Marjorie Coffey, USA, showing hand couched synthetic threads. (See colour photograph opposite page 65.)*

126. *Details from the orphrey of a cope for Chester Cathedral – By Judy Barry and Beryl Patten – 1981 colours red, gold and orange, design based on corn – And cerice, pinks, reds and mauves for the design based on pomegranate tree – showing Irish, Cornely and Bernina machine embroidery. (See also (4) and colour photograph opposite page 97.)*

127. *White and gold super frontal, 1980. One of set of four showing machine embroidery and collage by Judy Barry and Beryl Patten for All Saints Church, Stand, Whitefield, Manchester.*

127A. *Purple super frontal.*

127B. *Green super frontal.*

127C. *Red super frontal.*

11

Corporate Projects and Repair Work

Groups of people, interested in embroidery, who meet together to produce vestments and soft furnishings for their places of worship are playing an increasingly important part in the life of the church.

In these times of change the products of their enterprise are really needed, and the value of this corporate work cannot be overemphasised, provided that the aim is to attain the highest possible standard of artistry – but there are problems requiring discussion and forward planning.

This movement is a part of the attempt to involve people in the whole life of the church, and those who are experienced or just interested in design, embroidery, dressmaking or tailoring have much to offer, but to attain co-ordination individual efforts needs to be tactfully but firmly organised. Amateurs can produce excellent vestments and furnishings when expert advice is available to point the way to a unified scheme, so that everything is planned as part of the whole.

With increasing prices and decreasing sources of supply, there is a real need for the work undertaken by embroidery groups, provided that it reaches professional standards of design and workmanship and fulfils its liturgical purpose satisfactorily. With this aim it is important that information regarding modern trends shall be available.

The selection of the right person to lead the group is the problem, this was discussed with the Revd. Peter Delaney who made the following observations. He pointed out that the church having a professional available to lead its group is indeed fortunate, as only a trained person understands the limitations of the craft, and is able to design. Important as it is, designing is only a part of the project, the leader is there to direct and guide; so that, to the participants, learning and the application becomes a pleasure, they see the work growing, encouraged by the leader, who has overall control.

In many parishes there has been the problem of people thinking that they can do it on their own and getting nowhere, and realising that the resultant failure could have been avoided had they had the help of a leader to show the way; one whose experience makes it possible to anticipate and prevent mistakes, which, if allowed to happen in embroidery are difficult to rectify.

The value of these corporate projects is for people to work together. Such an undertaking is a microcosm of what the Christian church is meant to be – where problems are shared and when expertise is given in terms of firm leadership by the trained person. But this leader should not totally dominate to the exclusion of the encouragement of initiative, instead the creative skills of those taking part in the scheme should be developed.

128. *Replacing a worn background fabric.*

Repair work

Many churches possess old embroideries, it is important that professional advice should be sought before any conservation or repair work is attempted. Nor should anything which might be interesting be thrown out, because pieces which seem old-fashioned now, may be good examples of their type, they should be carefully stored away until a time comes when they will be re-appraised and appreciated.

Ancient pieces must be professionally restored. Straightforward repairs can be undertaken by a knowledgeable and technically good needlewoman. Usually it is the background which has worn, in many cases this can be renewed in the following way. Taking a mounted altar frontal as an example, first spread it out flatly, put over it a large sheet of cellofilm, and trace all round the outline of the embroidery.

Frame-up the new backing and the replacement fabric. Having pricked the outline of the design, transfer it to the background and paint it in. Cut out the units of embroidery and pin them in place upon the new background (128) and tack. Stitch round the edges, and with invisible stitches attach the whole area of the motif being applied. Using imagination, plan an extension to some of the lines, so that the finished result will be softened, sew down fine cords and/or couched threads to neaten the cut edges. Small details will have to be re-embroidered, and rays and spangles, etc., added. When complete, the lining can be replaced.

When the background silk has perished and it has been decided to repair and reinforce instead of renewing it entirely a different method is employed. To do this, first remove the lining anf interlining and frame up the backing and embroidery. The worn areas are reinforced with many rows of tramming, this consists of long, laid stitches in very fine, untwisted self-coloured floss silk (129), the laid threads are about $\frac{1}{2}$ cm apart, and are tied down with tiny stitches which are bricked with those of the previous row. When complete, the lining is replaced.

During the repair of old pieces it is essential that as little of the original stitchery as possible is removed.

Conservation is a specialised subject and should not be attempted without advice. Refer to the Bibliography for details of the book 'Caring for Textiles'.

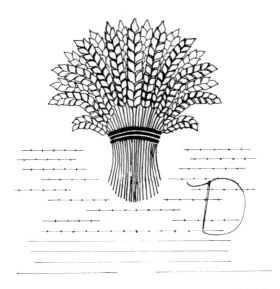

129. Repairing by tramming, a worn background fabric.

130. St Cuthbert's Maniple, worked in silk with a gold background.
Early tenth Century. The Treasury, Durham Cathedral.
(Photo: Courtesy of Dean & Chapter of Durham.)

12

A Brief Historical Sequence

In earlier times the church was the inspiration for man's greatest creativity and before that, in pagan worship. This is exemplified in the architecture of the Gothic cathedrals, sculpture, painting, stone carving, silversmithing, illuminated manuscripts, enamelling and embroidery. This flowering of all the medieval arts is almost impossible to recapture in imagination as we usually see individual pieces which are seldom in the colourful splendour of their original ambient.

Our interest is mainly in English embroidery, although it did not exist in isolation, it was known to surpass in excellence other work of the time. It must be considered in context and compared, for example, with the coronation mantle created in Sicily for Roger II in 1133 which is now in Vienna. Nor should we overlook the impact upon the Crusaders of the riches, both spiritual and temporal, of the Byzantine Empire, bringing back, as many no doubt did, treasured examples of textiles and embroideries.

In England there must have been an already established tradition of fine workmanship when St Cuthbert's stole and maniple were produced between 909 and 916, which are now in the Treasury of Durham Cathedral (130).

The designs during the great period of English church embroidery, Opus Anglicanum, 1250–1350 fall into three groups. The earliest type was formed from the spiralling of the vine, the tree of Jesse, which enclosed representations of saints identified by their symbols. The fabric used was generally rose coloured silk twill, as for the Jesse cope in the V & A museum.

Towards the end of the thirteenth century the basis of the design underwent a change. The ground was divided into circles (e.g. Ascoli Piceno cope), squares (131) (e.g. Steeple Aston dossal and frontal) or quatrefoils, e.g. the Syon cope also in the V & A museum; they contained the figures of saints or six-winged angels. The ground fabric was of blue, crimson or ivory silk or was entirely covered with gold, stitched to form patterns or embroidered in silk.

The third type of design (first half of the fourteenth century) was developed from the radiating arrangement of arcading, sometimes foliated, and with animals, birds or symbols filling the spandrels. The sacred figures within the arches were single or

131. Detail from the Steeple Aston Dossal and Frontal. V and A Museum.

grouped. Most usually crimson velvet was the material used; as in the Butler-Bowden cope (V & A Museum) (132).

Narrative subjects are common to most of the decoration at this time, because it was a way of teaching the Bible stories to the unlettered laity. Therefore the drawing of the gestures was exaggerated in order that the meaning might be clearly conveyed.

To work this embroidery a linen backing would have been framed up and over it was stitched the silk background fabric, but when the entire surface was to be embroidered, a finer linen formed the second layer.

Typical of the representations of this period are the high, broad foreheads and very large eyes, which can be seen in the detail (8, *page 26*) for these and all the silk work fine split-stitch was used, for the features it followed the outline, but on the cheeks it went round in spirals. The hair and beards were usually carried out in stripes of blue and white or yellow and reddish-brown. For the drapery of the garments the rows of stitches ran with the line of the folds, the darker tone on the outside, generally blue, green, reddish-brown or ivory. Sometimes an area of an open laid filling can be found and when there are fairly large areas of gold background these are stitched to form a pattern.

Certain details were first covered with stitchery and then entirely sewn with tiny seed pearls.

Another characteristic of Opus Anglicanum is the working of the metal threads, which was only possible because of the purity of the gold which made it pliant. For this method, known as underside couching, the gold thread lies on the surface, and the needle, threaded with a fine linen thread, is brought up through the fabric, and is then taken over the gold, and returned down through the same hole, which draws a little loop of gold through to the reverse side. For the succeeding rows the stitches alternate with those of the previous row. It is this gold work method which has contributed to the durability of the vestments.

The general standard of excellence both in the design and in the technique of embroidery deteriorated. The figures became squat and the drawing of the arcading clumsy. This decline was due, in part, to the Black Death and then to the Hundred Years' War, when gold became very costly. And at this time the introduction from Italy of new and more splendid woven velvet brocades deflected creativity away from embroidered decoration.

The splendid Company Palls belong to this time.

But later there was a revival of interest in the production of embroidered ecclesiastical vestments. It was a very different style which emerged, the design of which displayed a certain poverty of inspiration, though it had a distinct character. The background fabric was generally velvet, on which were applied isolated embroidered motifs, the subjects more often repeated were, the Virgin Mary surrounded by six-winged angels or the Crucifixion and there were also fleur de lis, Lantern flowers (133), double-headed eagles together with representations of the donors, their arms or puns upon their names.

These units were worked separately on linen, mainly in long and short stitch using floss silk, and there was some appliqué, the gold threads were laid on the surface and couched. When completed, each was cut out, and sewn to the background, then outlined. The hardness was countered by the addition of golden rays and spangles.

Many of these fifteenth century vestments remain. The copes generally had a central motif at the back with smaller ones sprinkled around. The hoods were large and edged with fringe. Frequently the hood and orphrey (and those upon chasubles) were composed of figure subjects and were of an earlier origin, frequently Flemish.

At the Reformation quantities of vestments were destroyed, some were burned for the gold and others converted for secular use. The jewels were removed. (Of those treasures which survived, many were damaged later by Cromwell's men.)

133. Dalmatic
– mid sixteenth century.
Cream silk damask
and red velvet.
One of the vestments
made for St Johns
College, Oxford,
which survived the
Reformation and
came to light in the
fourteenth century.
(Photo:
Birmingham Museums
& Art Gallery.)

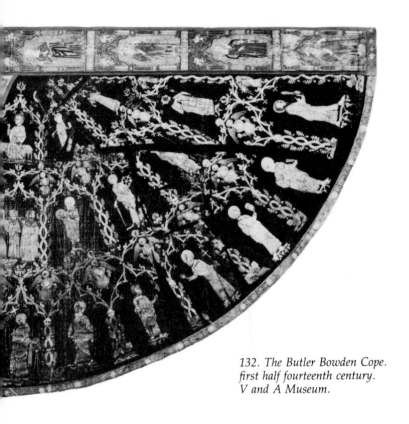

132. *The Butler Bowden Cope.*
first half fourteenth century.
V and A Museum.

Some of the families who continued in the Roman Catholic faith hid away vestments for the priest's wear during the secret celebrations of the Mass.

In the newly established Church of England the wearing of vestment's was forbidden, but in some cathedrals and churches cope were still worn, in the Treasury of Durham Cathedral are three such examples. And at Westminster Abbey are the red, green and 'purplish black' sets of velvet copes (the white have worn out) made for the coronation of Charles II. The design of the silver embroidered decoration is excellent and the techniques used are interesting, much of it is raised, and the silver plate has been passed backwards and forwards across the shapes, textured gold and silver cords, and spangles give variety. Basket fillings have been included (134).

Altar frontals continued to be used, at Axbridge, Somerset there is a unique example, carried out in canvas work and made to fit over the altar, it was completed in 1720. On the front between the twisted columns, the design shows a contemporary communion table, set for the celebration of the Eucharist. On the top is worked the sacred monogram placed in the circle of eternity, and with flames shooting out in all directions. It suggests the 'Sun of Righteousness'. This symbol was very popular in the seventeenth and eighteenth centuries, and was frequently embroidered with metal threads upon velvet.

Embroidered bookbindings continued to be worked in a variety of techniques, the British Museum possesses several examples.

Ladies of leisure have always taken pleasure in stitching for the church, one such example, of particular interest, comes from Weston Favell, Northamptonshire, is dated 1698 and shows the Last Supper (135). The whole background is sewn with bugle beads. In the nineteenth century some of the amateur embroidery was hardly worthy of its purpose and the influence exerted by the Pre-Raphaelite movement came at just the right time. The stained glass of Burne Jones inspired designs for embroidery, this led to long and short stitch, stem stitch and split stitch worked with filo-floss and untwisted floss being employed to the exclusion of almost all other stitches (136). But May Morris used more subtle colours and worked with twisted silks upon fine wool or linen.

Gradually, vestments had been re-introduced, due in part to the Gothic Revival and to the influence of Dr Percy Dearmer. The longer, fuller chasuble replaced the cut away, abbreviated form. But at the beginning of the twentieth century, design for church embroidery became old-fashioned and the ideas outworn.

The decorative styles of each historical period are reflected in

134. *One of the set of Red Copes, seventeenth century. Westminster Abbey.*

134A. *Detail of one of the set of Black Copes. Westminster Abbey.*

175

the development of vestment design (11); in particular the Roman Catholic countries of Europe. Examples are exhibited in the collections of the Treasury at St Peters, Rome, the Vatican Museum and also in the museums on the Continent, Britain and America.

But in those countries most changed by the Reformation and specially in Britain where the influence of the Puritans was strong, the excessive flamboyance of the Baroque and Rococo decoration made but little impression, as, at that time vestments were not generally worn.

We are living in an exciting time of change – a coming together of many influences in a widespread renewal of the sacred arts; not since the sixteenth century has there been such a calling in question of received traditions.

The Liturgical movement on the continent of the 1930s has stimulated fresh thought and understanding, it is among continental Roman Catholics that the signs of renewal are most apparent, but this influence has taken time to permeate to the visual arts, such as embroidery. As a result it is gradually becom-

135. 'The Last Supper'. The background is composed of bugle beads. 17th century. The Parish Church of St Peter Westom Favell, Northampton. (Photo: Peter Gadd.)

136. Altar Frontal, designed by William Morris. Probably worked by the 'Leek Embroidery Society', nineteenth century. Cheddleton, Leek, Staffordshire. (Photo: Kenneth Edwards, Leek.)

ing understood that all decoration should be related to Liturgical function; so that it never becomes an end in itself.

Design for embroidery in Britain had become old-fashioned, and dull, outworn symbols were endlessly repeated and all impact was lost, this continued until forward looking artists who understood the requirements of the Liturgical movement tried to infuse new vitality into symbolic forms which had lost all meaning and reference.

To have lived at the time when Le Corbusier's chapel of pilgrimage at Ronchamp and the Matisse chapel at Vence were completed and to have witnessed the creation of the church of St Paul, Bow Common, London by Robert Maguire have been stimulating experiences, which not only revealed the importance of Liturgical function but established that 'sacred art has always demanded a certain degree of abstraction, purging it of the sentimental and literary irrelevancies which obscured its essential function', to quote the Revd Peter Hammond.

Interesting vestments of good, up-to-date design, made of variously woven textiles, were being produced in Germany, Holland and France before this influence was felt in other countries.

177

Three-dimensional decorative head inspired by a gargoyle, made with suede and leather, by Sheila Berry.

Bibliography

Child, Heather and Colles, Dorothy. Christian Symbols. Bell, 1971.

Christie, A. G. I. English Medieval Embroidery. Oxford, 1938.

Ireland, Marion P. Textile Art in the Church. Abingdon Press, Nashville and New York, 1966.

Finch and Putnam. Caring for Textiles. Barrie and Jenkins, 1977.

Russell, Pat. Lettering for Embroidery. Batsford, 1971.

Bishop's Committee on the Liturgy, Environment and Art in Catholic Worship.

National Conference of Catholic Bishops, 1978. Washington, D.C.

Heim, Bruno Berne. Heraldry in the Catholic Church. Van Duren, 1978.

Dawson, Barbara. Metal Thread Embroidery. Batsford, 1976.

Roeder, Helen. Saints and their Attributes. Longmans Green, 1955.

Milburn, R. L. P. Saints and their Emblems in English Churches. Blackwell, 1957.

Green, Sylvia. Canvas Embroidery for Beginners. Studio Vista, 1970.

Green, Sylvia. Patchwork for Beginners. Studio Vista, 1971.

Dean, Beryl. Creative Appliqué. Studio Vista, 1970.

Dean, Beryl. Ecclesiastical Embroidery. Batsford, 1958.

Dean, Beryl. Church Neddlework. Batsford, 1961.

Dean, Beryl. Ideas for Church Embroidery. Batsford, 1968.

Dean, Beryl. Embroidery in Religion and Ceremonial. Batsford, 1981.

Coleman, A. The Creative Sewing Machine. Batsford.

Clucas, J. Your Machine for Embroidery. Bell-Machine Embroidery. English Sewing, 56 Oxford St., Manchester.

Suppliers of Materials

Allans, 55–56 Duke Street, Grosvenor Sq., London W1M 6HS. Exclusive fabrics.

Ells and Farrier, 5 Princes St., Hanover Sq., London W1. Jewels, Beads and Sequins.

John, V. D. KilBride, Ditchling Common, Hassocks, Sussex BN6 8TP. Handloom woven silks and silk/cotton cloth in Liturgical colours, 60 inches wide, therefore copes and chasubles can be cut without joins. These interesting fabrics hang beautifully. Visitors are welcome.

John Lewis, Oxford St., London W1. Wadding, interfacing, threads, piping cords, etc.

MacCulloch and Wallis Ltd., 25–26 Dering St., London W1R 0BH. Dowlas linen, interlining. Rubber solution, fabric adhesive, vanishing muslim, interfacing.

Mace and Nairn, 89 Crane St., Salisbury, Wiltshire SP1 2PY. Embroidery specialists, metal threads, cords, canvas, threads and linen, etc.

Liberty and Co. Ltd., Regent St., London W1. Some Thai silks and Indian silks, other fabrics.

Reeves-Dryad Ltd., 178 Kensington High St., London W8. Felt and other supplies and papers.

Royal School of Needlework, 25 Princes Gate, London SW7. Metal threads, gold and silver cords, silk cords, canvas, wools, etc.

Watts and Co. Ltd., 7 Tufton St., London SW1. Church Furnishers. Cloth of gold and substitutes, braids, cords, etc.

Lilliman and Cox Ltd., 34 Bruton Place, London W1. Specialists in dry cleaning.

Embroiderers' Guild (members only), Apartment 41 A, Hampton Court Palace, East Molesey, Surrey. Advice, Books, Collection historical and embroideries. Classes. Publishers of 'Embroidery' quarterly.

Index

(References are to page numbers)

Adhesive, 121
Alms bags, 72
Altar cushions, 75
    frontals, 53, 174
Ambo fall, 58
Amice, 86
Appliqué, 119
Aumbrey curtain, 67

Backing, 31, 101, 170
Banners, 66
Blind hem stitch (machine), 156, 160
Bonding, 156, 161
Book covers, 78, 174
Braiding, 157
Broderie Anglaise, 90
Burse, 68

Canvas, 146, 147, 173
Cassock-alb, 30, 31
Chasuble, 21, 24–35, 175
Circle, 15
Collar, 31, 33
Colour, 21
Cope, 13, 40, 124
Cords, 111
Corporal, 84
Corporate projects, 7, 165, 166
Cotta, 86
Couching, 105–9, 167, 172
Credence cloth, 84
Crosses, 17, 19
Cushions, 146–52 (*see also* Altar)

Dalmatic, 39
Desk fall, 58
Dye, 155, 161

Enlarging, 10

Fabric marking pens, 119, 154
Fabrics, 30, 124, 125, 129
Facing, 33–4, 83
Fair linen cloth, 83
Falls, 58

Framing up, 100, 103, 119, 121, 131–2, 166
Fringes, 138
Frontals, 53, 57

Hand-worked linen, 90
Hangings, 70
Hemstitch, 83, 123
Hoods, 46, 173

Interlining, 33, 121, 125, 156, 159, 167

Japanese gold, 105–9

Kneelers, 146–52

Laid work, 141, 167–72
Lavabo towels, 85
Leaders, 147
Lectern fall, 58
Lighting, 22
Liturgical colours, 121

Machine embroidery, 153–64
Mantle, 169
Metal threads, 105
Mitre, 47
Mola, 128

Needle weaving, 143

Opus Anglicanum, 169
Orphrey, 13, 29, 173

Padding, 110–11, 115
Pall, 85
Passing thread, 110, 114–15
Patchwork, 124
Piping, 77
Plate, 114–15
Pressing, 161
Puckering, 121, 151, 154
Pulpit fall, 58
Purificator, 85
Purl (check, bead) 111, 114–15, 142

Quilting, 119

Reducing, 10
Repairs, 165–8
Resurrection, 15
Richelieu, 91

Saints, 17
Sling, 108–11
Stitches –
  Algerian Eye, 148
  Back, 119, 132
  Basket, 107
  Buttonhole, 133, 141
  Ceylon, 134, 141
  Chain, 136–7
  Chevron, 132
  Cloud filling, 141
  Counted thread satin stitches,
    94
  Cretan, 134
  Cross, 150
  Double Smyrna, 132
  Encroaching Goblin, 148
  Eye, 148
  Faggot, 92, 95
  Feather, 134
  Fern, 132
  Fishbone, 132
  Florentine, 148
  Fly, 134
  Hemming, 129
  Herringbone, 121, 132
  Hungarian, 151
  Interlaced band, 139
  Knotted stitches, 137–8

Ladder, 134
Long and short, 29, 132, 173
Pekinese, 139
Pin, 96
Plaited Gobelin, 151
Raised chainband, 115, 139
Rice, 151
Rope, 134
Roumanian, 132
Satin, 132
Seeding, 94, 132
Slip stitching, 83, 123
Smyrna Cross, 150
Split, 29, 132, 170, 173
Stem, 132
Straight cross, 148
Tent, 148
Trailing, 93–4
Turkey knots, 148
Upright Gobelin, 148
Velvet, 148
Wave, 141
Stoles, 35, 169
Stretching, 151
Surplice cotta, 86
Symbols, 15–20, 175

Thread, 141, 147, 153
Tramming, 167
Transferring, 99, 119, 121, 147, 166
Tree of Life, 15
Tunicle, 39

Veil, 68
Vestments, 21, 24, 171, 173